Gainful Gardens in Florida

Learn How To Grow Anything You Want In Your Florida Climate

Maxwell P. Diwa

Contents

Part Three
Vegetables

Part Four
Nuts, Herbs, and Miscellaneous

Part Five
Rooting Hormone

Introduction

Gardening has always been a popular hobby for millions of people worldwide. However, with the rising costs of living, gardening has grown in popularity and has changed from simply being a hobby to becoming an entire way of life. Now, not only are individuals growing the odd fruit and vegetable but they are devoting larger spaces to their backyards to grow more food so as not to have to buy them from the supermarkets.

Unfortunately, there are still some that are hesitant to begin such a hobby. This hesitation comes from how complicated gardening seems. To be successful in gardening there are a number of factors that come into play: sun exposure, soil richness, plant companions, and the list goes on. To make matters more complicated, these variables change based on your location and climate. In fact in some areas, where you would think growing would be ideal, gardening becomes more complicated.

For example, gardening in Florida can be a tricky task as the soil is much more sandy than expected, and the climate is more unpredictable. This means that the balancing of these variables requires more patience and finesse. Of course you already know this, or you would not have picked up this book.

Wouldn't it be nice if there was a book that had everything you needed to know to begin a successful and fruitful garden in the Florida climate? This is where this book comes in. Within these pages you will find tips, tricks, and how-to's to grow your own food in Florida.

There is quite a lot of information when it comes to gardening, let alone gardening in Florida. For this reason we have divided the book into five carefully researched parts. The first part will just talk about the basics of what you need to know to have a bountiful harvest every year.

The next three parts- 2,3, and 4-,are dedicated to a specific food category: fruits, vegetables, and, nuts, herbs, and miscellaneous. The fifth and final part will provide some recipes for homemade fertilizers and pest deterrents.

Whether you are looking for a small garden to have in the warmer months, or if you're looking for a year-round self-sustaining garden, this book gives you everything you need to know and to use as reference to have a bountiful and fruitful garden.

Without further ado let's get started!

Part One

Gardening Basics

Chapter 1

Gardening Basics

Chapter Introduction

Before we move to the specifics of how you can have a successful garden in the Florida climate, you should first know how the basics of gardening work.

Let's go through some tips and tricks on how to have a successful garden in general and a list of some of the tools to make that happen.

Tools For Your Garden

No matter if you have a garden in your backyard, on the roof, in your home, or have an entire homestead, you will need mostly the same tools (Millcreek Garden, 2018).

- Soil

There is a common misunderstanding that soil is just dirt. It's not. Soil is a kind of ecosystem or active collection of nutrients and vitamins - in addition to dirt - that helps your plants to grow.

- Hoe

This is a tool with a long handle and a piece of metal or plastic at the end. The end is a flat and sharp surface that helps to push soil out of the way and to pull weeds out of the garden.

- Rake

A rake, and its long finger-like tips, is a great tool to have in your garden. It can be used to mix the soil, distribute seeds and fertilizers, and gather weeds and leaves quickly. Although a rake isn't necessary, it is a rather useful tool to have in your garden arsenal.

- Shovel

You will need multiple shovels. One for digging large holes, deeper into the ground, and a few smaller ones to dig shallow holes for smaller plants. Thankfully, these usually come in sets of different sizes.

- Trowel

This is a smaller shovel. It can be incredibly useful for potted plants or planting smaller plants into garden beds.

- Gloves

You are going to get dirty- that is just a fact of gardening. To protect your hands from getting too dirty, or to protect them from sharp edges, stems and thorns, or harmful chemicals, gloves are a must have in your tool kits.

- Water

You will need a water source to make sure that your plants and soil don't dry out too much. Usually you will be getting water from the rain, but in the case of warmer weather or heat spells and droughts, you will want another source of water to make sure you can supplement your garden.

- Knee Pads

Knee pads are not a necessity but they sure come in handy when you are crouching and kneeling for long periods of time. Unless you have all of your gardens in tall raised beds that are waist high, you are going to need to kneel. Knee pads can help to protect your knees.

- Outdoor Protection

This includes things like water for yourself, closed toe shoes, a hat, and sunscreen. Unless all of your gardens are inside, you are going to need to protect yourself from outdoor elements when you garden.

- Sunlight

Plants need sunlight to grow and absorb nutrients. Although you can't really bring the sun to the plants, you can bring the plants to the sun. Make sure your plants are in a place where the sun hits for about 6 hours a day. If not, make sure your plants are moveable so you can move them around to follow the sun.

Indeed some plants grow better in shade, but most of them need about 6 hours of sunlight per day.

- Thermometer

Even though most plants love a lot of sunlight, it is possible for the plants to become too hot. Having a thermometer to help you tell how hot it is can give you clues as to how to treat your plants. Do you need to bring them inside? Or do you need to water them more?

- Steaks

Some plants need help to grow upwards. For instance, vines, or tomato and cucumber plants need help and support to continue to grow. Having steaks, trellises, or lattice can help your plant grow big and strong.

- Lumber and Building Materials

You will need all sorts of building supplies like screws, nails, and lumber to help add borders to your garden or make raised beds.

How to Start A Garden- What You Really Need To Know

Now that we have all of the tools we need, let's look at the steps needed to make a successful garden Here are the basics (Neverman, 2022).

1. Choose What To Grow

The first step to gardening is choosing what you want to grow. This is the first step because depending on your answer how you garden, where you garden, and how you care for your garden is going to differ.

Generally you have three choices. You can grow edible plants, you can grow non-edible plants, or you can grow a combination of both. If you're growing plants for decorative purposes all you really need to focus on is whether or not they are shade loving plants or sun loving plants. Of course this book is focused on growing edible plants and the choice for that is a little bit more complicated.

You want to make sure that what you are planting is food- fruits, vegetables, herbs, etc., that you are going to eat. If you don't eat the food in your regular everyday life it is highly suggested that you don't even try to plant it. It would only lead to you taking up space in your garden for food that you would rather eat.

It's also important to choose what you want to plant because it will dictate the size of your garden and where you put it. For example if you are growing vegetables like potatoes, zucchini, and squash, then plant them in the ground. If you are planting things like lettuce or tomatoes, you might want to plant them in a raised bed. It will also dictate whether or not you need a support system or if your entire garden can come indoors. For instance, if you are planting just an herb garden, most people like to keep it indoors so they can better control how their herbs grow.

All of this is to say the first step in creating a garden is to list all of the plants that you want to grow. From there we can move to the next step.

2. Pick a location

After you know what you're gardening, then you're going to want to pick your location. Again this decision starts with a choice between two options: inside or outside. This will depend on how big your space is inside, how big of a yard you have, and what you're growing.

Again, for the purposes of this book, we will focus more on outdoor growth so that's what we're going to focus on here in this stuff as well. Once you choose outside you're going to want to wait a few days to track the sun's movement. Pay attention to which part of your yard gets the most sun, which part of your yard gets sun for around six hours, and which part of your yard is mostly shaded.

Indeed most plants require some sort of sunlight, however the amount of sunlight is crucial as certain plants are very picky. Depending on the soil type and the plant you may want more shade or less shade. Some plants like the morning sun while others enjoy the afternoon sun.

The sunlight specifications for any plant are usually written on a card once you purchase the plant: We will also be going through the sunlight specifications for the different fruits and vegetables in this book. But before you begin that step, you need to understand your yard. You need to find which location you're going to plant, which type of vegetables, and what part of your yard you're just going to leave alone.

3. Plan Your Garden

Now it's time to plan your garden. Figure out which plants grow best with others and which plants are not to be grown together at all. Decide which plants are growing directly into the ground, which can be grown in pots, and which are going to be grown in garden beds.

Once you have all of these specifications you can draw a blueprint of what you want your garden to look like. For many this is a tedious task but it will help you in the long run to get a fruitful and bountiful harvest.

You should take into account walkways and the general set up of your yard in relation to where you want to plant. It will also allow you to visualize the garden before planting. You will be able to see if something fits or does not fit in the space that you want it to. Moving a garden bed is much easier done when it is empty than when it is full of soil and plants.

It doesn't have to be a fully rendered image. But the general blueprint can go a long way in relieving much of the stress that comes with gardening and beginning a garden specifically.

4. Buy and Gather Tools

Before you even think about gardening you have to make sure you have all of the right tools. This includes making sure you have enough gloves, shovels, and water sources available. But this also means that you should build all of your garden beds first.

Have everything laid out and ready before you purchase or get your plants. It may be a while until you feel like the garden bed, but having it ready for you will save a lot of time in the long run.

Take a look at the above list of tools to make sure that your collection is complete.

5. Test A Sample of Your Soil

Most individuals skip this step and use the trial and error method of planting: that is when they simply plant into the ground and wait to see what grows. While this is generally effective, it costs time and money. Not to mention you nearly have to wait two years to really know what grows best where.

One way to avoid this trial-and-error method is to test your soil. Testing your soil will help you determine if your soil is more acidic, more neutral, or alkaline. It can also tell you what kind of bugs or chemicals are in your soil due to local pollution or waterways. Samples can tell you if you have clay or rocks or a mixture of different soil types within your ground.

All of this information is important because it can help you determine what to grow. Usually crops and plants prefer a soil that has a pH around 7- or that is neutral. That being said, a plant like potatoes prefers more acidic soil.

It's important to test your soil then to cross-reference your results with the list of things that you want to grow. Make sure that what you want to grow is compatible with your soil type and if not make sure you take the steps to fix any issues.

6. Prep The Soil

The next step is to prepare your soil for planting. You're going to want to put down a barrier between your grass or your ground and your soil. This is usually some sort of fertilizer or mulch to help keep the moisture within the soil and help give the soil nutrients overtime. Of course you can purchase mulch but lining your grass with newspaper before you put your soil down will also do just as well.

You might want to think about getting some bone meals or other types of plant fertilizer to help prep the soil as well. Be sure to water the soil to moisten it before you plant it. You never want to put your plant into completely dry soil.

Be sure to fill any beds you have with soil to make sure that you have enough and you will be able to dig deep enough to plant any fruit or vegetable.

Essentially this step is mainly just making sure your soil is as ready as possible for planting. There are a lot of things that can go wrong in the planting and growing process so trying to prep your soil as best as possible will give you the best chance of having a successful garden.

7. Collect the Seeds, Propagated, or Transplanted Plants

Once you have prep your soil it's now time to gather the plants. There are a few different ways that you can start planting.

First, you can plant the seeds. Almost every fruit and vegetable will have a seed of some sort that you can begin to grow from. Most of these seeds will need to be started indoors and in small amounts of water and soil. Playing something from Steve can also be rather time-consuming as the roots will need to be established. However, it is one of the more cost-effective ways of gardening because it's usually cheaper.

Another way to begin is to plant propagated plants. These are plants that are usually regrown from scraps. Instead of throwing out the leftovers or the stems of the fruit of the vegetable, someone can take care of them and begin the regrowth process. At this point you would just take the propagated plant and plant it in the garden appropriately. This is the more cost-effective way since you can propagate the food that you eat at your own home and regrow it yourself. Unfortunately when you use these types of cuttings sometimes your regrowth isn't as large as if you were to grow it from a seed.

Your final option when it comes to planting is to transplant already existing or already started plants. Usually you can get these from a garden center or even from a grocery store. Essentially what it is that someone took the time to grow and begin the growth process from the seed. Usually as long as these plants are cared for they can last forever and won't have to be replanted every season. Again, this can be a more expensive option, however, because you still have to purchase the plants.

8. Plant Carefully

Now that we have gathered everything we need, and have prepared everything we need to prepare, it is time to plant. We can't just plant whatever we want however we want. You need to acclimate your plants to your specific climate and then plant according to the companionship.

Although the climate for a specific city is generally the same, your climate, in your backyard, can change ever so slightly from the climate in your neighbors. For example, perhaps your yard gets more sunlight or more wind than your neighbors do. Experts say that simply keeping your plant outside in your pots before you plant - just for a few days - can help acclimate it to your specific climate before you plant. This way you will have a better chance of the roots establishing themselves.

You also want to pay attention to the companionship of your plants. Certain plants do not grow well with others, while other pairs help to fertilize each other very well and encourage growth.

We will include a chart of general plant companionship in this book, but it would be wise for you to look into the specific growth companions for every one of your plants. Indeed it may take some time and a little bit more effort however it will better your chances of having a bountiful harvest.

Lastly, you don't want to plant aggressively. Take care of the plant and make sure that you are placing them in the soil deliberately but gently. You don't want to damage any leaves or the structure of the plant itself.

9. Care For The Garden

Now that everything is planted and settled it's time to care for and nurture your garden. Really, this is the fun part of gardening. You get to go out daily and make sure that your plants are growing as they should. You get to watch as they mature, flower, and eventually bear the fruit or vegetables that you intend to grow.

Although this is usually the fun part, it can take a lot of effort. You have to make sure that your gardens are getting enough water. This means you may have to water them yourselves if you don't get enough rain. Generally, about an inch of water every few days should be sufficient, but make sure that you double check with your plant specific watering needs.

Fertilize regularly and watch for pests and animals. The more pests that you have the more likely that your fruit will either be eaten or it will rot.

Even with this work, caring for your garden is what is incredibly rewarding about the process. You can literally watch something grow.

10. Harvest

After a significant amount of effort you get to reap the rewards, and harvest and pick the fruits and vegetables that you've grown. While this is an incredibly rewarding and tasty part of the gardening process, it does take a very careful hand and eye.

Different plants will mature at different times of the year and have different brightness qualities. Some of them will stay right until you pick them while others will begin to rot if they aren't chosen at the right time.

Pay attention to the ripeness cues that your plans are giving you. You may even want to keep a journal or a calendar letting you know when certain harvesting seasons and time are coming up.

Don't feel pressured to pick everything all at once, nor should you feel pressured to only pick a little bit at a time. Pick what you want, but make sure it's enough to maintain a healthy crop. Some crops need you to pick their fruits often and some new fruits can grow. You can always freeze or preserve the food if you pick too much.

The Bottom Line

The bottom line is that gardening is one of the most rewarding hobbies or pastimes that you can have. For one part you are watching something and helping something grow. On the other hand, your hobby can help feed and nurture your own family. That being said, it is one that takes a significant amount of time and effort to do well and to do successfully.

There are a lot of different parts to gardening so making sure they are all inline is most important.

While the beginning steps are generally the same, growing in different climates and areas requires some specific steps and changes to the process.

Chapter 2

Gardening In Florida

Chapter Introduction

Although it would seem like everything is coming out of Florida and therefore can be grown in Florida, gardening in the southern state can be difficult. Now that we have gone through some of the basics that you need to know to be a successful Gardener, it's now time to look at some of the specific issues and gardening techniques you will need to know in order to have a successful garden in Florida.

Why Is Gardening In Florida Tricky?

Florida Gardening Challenges #1: It's Hot

Did you know that in the summer months Florida is closer to the Sun? This makes the temperature a lot higher. As a result, crops that enjoy cooler temperatures suffer from smaller harvests and may die out. Therefore, when people in other states begin their gardening seasons in the summer, those of us in Florida may want to garden in either the spring, the fall or even the winter months (Annie, 2017).

Florida Gardening Challenges #2: The Soil Is Not Soil

Yes, technically the soil in Florida is soil. Yet if we get down to the specifics, the soil is really sand. This means that you have to add more nutrients and care for your soil more in order for it to help you yield crops. Alternatively, you have to purchase proper gardening soil and have all of your plants in actual beds rather than planting them directly in the ground. This can increase the cost and effort associated with gardening.

Florida Gardening Challenges #3: More Soil Issues

The soil not being soil is the only problem. But it is a problem that leads to a more serious one. Anything that you put in the soil to help make it more nutrient-rich seems to disappear. This means that each season, if you are planting into the ground, you will have to continuously put in more fertilizers and more growth feed.

Florida Gardening Challenges #4: Nutrients, Nutrients, Nutrients!

On account of the fact that the nutrients don't stay in the soil, you will need to provide and give the nutrients to the soil and not only on a constant basis but in a variety of different ways. You will need to have compost, fertilizers, growth stimulants, and maybe even manure available to you in order to truly enrich the sand (Annie, 2017).

Florida Gardening Challenges #5: Bugs and Pest and Animals, Oh My!

Dealing with bugs, pests, and small animals that eat your Harvest is one of the downfalls of gardening in general. However, it would seem that in Florida the number of these pests have multiplied. Due to the hot weather bugs speak shade within your plants and small animals help themselves to dinner. This means that you will have to be more diligent with your pest control and perhaps even spend a little bit of money to invest in animal deterrents.

Florida Gardening Challenges #6: Temperamental Temperature

Indeed the Florida climate is hot. But it is not hot consistently. Just as soon as you get used to 1 kind of temperature the climate will shift and it will be raining for a significant amount of time; or windy: or on seasonably cold.

Not only do these shifts and temperature change seasonally but they can change within the same day. Such changes can make the task of gardening more difficult. You can't count on any sort of climate. Even if the weather says it's going to rain you should still be prepared to water your garden yourself. Even if it says it's sunny, be prepared to stay inside in case there is a torrential downpour.

Florida Gardening Challenges #7: Wasted Water

Again moving back to the soil, it does not hold water well. This means that more water will likely need to be used for your plans to absorb a sufficient amount. To make matters worse with such a hot climate, if you water after a full day of squelching heat you're likely to burn the plants with the water. This means that not only do you have to be careful of how much water you give to your plants but you also have to be careful of the time you take care of your plants. In the evening it is better.

Florida Gardening Challenges #8: Indestructible Weeds

Just as the pests seem more vicious in Florida, so do the weeds. While some weeds are decorative and pretty, making them not quite so undesirable to be around, most weeds will get in your way and need to be removed. This will prove in itself to be a difficult task. In order to truly kill the weed you will have to either dig it up entirely from the roots or put some sort of plant killer on them. Of course if you do this latter option then you have to be careful because you don't want to poison your own crops. When it comes to weeding in Florida, try to work with as many people as you can and be incredibly diligent and careful with the ones you take away.

Florida Gardening Challenges #9: Terrifying Tools

Again, the heat can be dangerous. Metal tools in the hot sun become dangerous weapons when it comes to gardening. In most cases, while you try to put your tools in a secure place, they're still likely going to heat up. This means that you either have to garden when it is cooler outside or you have to invest in tools that do not have metal ends but rather plastic ones or rubber. Unfortunately these tools can be slightly more expensive or less effective in their jobs.

Florida Gardening Challenges #10: Plenty Of Prep

One last challenge when it comes to gardening and planting in Florida is not the prep that has to go into the garden but the prep that you yourself have to go through in order to go outside. Sunscreen, water, a hat, and the appropriate clothing are just some of the necessities. You will also need bug spray and all of your tools (Annie, 2017).

With these challenges it may seem like gardening in Florida may be a chore instead of an enjoyable and rewarding hobby. Don't let these challenges fool you, most fruits, vegetables and foods grow incredibly well in Florida. You will only need to make your garden 'Florida Friendly.'

Being Florida Friendly

Being "Florida Friendly" means that you simply garden keeping in mind all of the specifics of the Florida climate, soil, and growing conditions.

Here are some tips on how to make your gardens more compatible with the growing conditions of the state.

Florida-Friendly Tip#1: Find the Right Place

Be sure you are putting the right plant in the right place in terms of sunlight, soil requirements, and companion plants. This way you will be working with the environment and not be forced to work against it, or change the natural preferences of the plant.

Florida-Friendly Tip#2: Water Correctly

It's easy to waste water when it comes to watering your gardens in Florida. Be sure you are using it to your advantage. You can make water reservoirs under or beside the soil that feed into the soil. This will help to curb the damage from the heat without wasting water. Also opting to water your gardens in the evening will allow your plants to absorb the water rather than be burned by it.

Florida-Friendly Tip#3: Fertilize!

To be clear, fertilizing is not a necessary practice when gardening. Many successful gardeners don't fertilize their plants. But if you want to have the best chance of having a bountiful and healthy garden, fertilizing is the way to go!

This doesn't mean that all fertilizers are one size fits all. Different plants have different needs. Moreover, different nutrients and fertilizers can be expensive. It is important that you do your research into which ones will work best for your plants.

You will also want to look into fertilizers that are dissolvable in water. This way you can mix your fertilizer with your water and use that water to hydrate and feed your plants in the evening.

Florida-Friendly Tip#4: Use Mulch

Mulch is an organic substance that helps to keep moisture and nutrients within the soil and not let it drain away quickly. Mulch is also a way to deter pests and animals while also shielding the base of your plants and its roots from the hot sun.

Mulch can be any organic material including shredded newspapers, leaves, sawdust, or commercially sold mulch. Investing in mulch for your gardens, especially in the Florida climate, will give your plants the best chance they have to yield a hardy harvest.

Florida-Friendly Tip#5: Attracting Animals

Generally you want to deter pests and wildlife from your yard. However, you do not want to read your garden completely of all insects and animals. Instead you want to strategically attract and defend your garden from certain animals. Insects like butterflies and bees are great for plant fertilization and pollination. Likewise certain basic insects and animals that don't harm your plants, will help you to deter other harmful insects.

You can install bird feeders or bird baths, and surround your vegetable and fruit crops with wild flowers that attract butterflies. This will help you get the good insects and animals while still allowing you to participate in the insect deterrent practices.

Florida-Friendly Tip#6: Be Responsible With Pest Control

Along the same lines of pest control, you have to be incredibly careful. You do not want to use a chemical that can also harm your plants; or even worse you do not want to use a chemical that can harm people.

Natural deterrents such as peppermint water, biodegradable soaps, or citrus peels can all help to keep unwanted bugs and insects away while still keeping your Harvest healthy. It is nearly impossible to rid your garden completely of insects and animals. Even if you were to move your garden completely indoors, insects will find their way in. The best you can do is simply to deter them from eating or harming your plants. Be wary not to get caught up in completely reading your garden and insects. You may end up harming yourself and your garden in general as a result.

Florida-Friendly Tip#7: Reuse and Recycle

You will likely need to rake, prune, and weed your gardens. Instead of throwing these away it would be wise of you to reuse these scraps in your garden. If you shred these scraps and use them as mulch or compost, and return them to the garden, you are reusing much of the same nutrients.

In general, recycle and reuse as many scraps as you can that you pull from the garden. Especially if they're healthy weeds or pruning from healthy plants. Clearly these plants are thriving in the garden so by reusing them as mulch or compost you are helping your other plants to absorb even more nutrients: without having to pay for more from the store.

In the end, you make your garden be Florida-friendly by tweaking the aforementioned basic rules of gardening. Now that we've gone through some of the general changes and specifications of gardening in Florida, let's look at some of the specifics that make Florida gardening so unique. Specifically, let's dive into the Florida climate, the soil in Florida, and the animals and pests that you may encounter.

Soil and Climate In Florida

Florida is separated into three geographical areas: south, north, and central. Each zone has its own specific soil, climate, and soil requirements (SL441/SS655).

Southern Florida Soil and Climate

The soil in the southern parts of Florida is the most nutrient rich in the state. This is thanks in part to the nutrient dense everglades that border the southern region. The soil is generally made up of peat, sand, rocks, marl and muck; these last two are soil substances that are high in fertilizers and nutrients. Unfortunately, even though the soil is high in nutrients it also has a high ph level. This means that the water and nutrients will wash away. The quick drainage, in addition to the sun in south Florida, means that you will want to water the plants often.

Central Florida Soil and Climate

You will get plenty of sun in this area so water retention is incredibly important. The soil tends to drain and lose water more quickly than other areas. This is because the soil is largely made up of sand, clay, and peat- a soil made up of vegetable matter. To plant successfully here, make sure you have enough water going into your soil to make up for the speed of loss. Since water takes with it any nutrients and moisture from the soil, you will also want to make sure that you add nutrients to the soil on a regular basis.

The climate is generally warm and subtropical. You shouldn't expect freezing temperatures but be prepared in case freezing does occur.

Northern Florida Soil and Climate

The soil in northern Florida is very similar to the soil found in central Florida. It is very sandy and has high water drainage. The difference is that this area is more prone to cooler temperatures. So while you treat the soil the same way you would in the central climate, you will also want to make sure you have heaters and tarps to protect the soil and plants from freezing.

Animals and Pests

Even though every plant is different, there are some bugs and pests that are common all over Florida for infiltrating gardens. You've got to know how to safely repel these pests to keep your crops safe (Climate - Florida).

- Caterpillars

Caterpillars are generally harmless to humans but they chew and eat leaves, and therefore can remove all the leaves from a variety of your crops. For some plants caterpillars can eat the flowers, stems, roots, and the actual fruit or vegetable. In this way they can be damaging to your crops. The best way to rid your plants of caterpillars is to pick them off your plants by hand. Other than that, you can spray your plants with different chemicals designed for caterpillar repellent. To rid your plant naturally you can spray your plants with a mixture of soapy water, water mixed with chili peppers, or water mixed with water and garlic. Use any spray sparingly.

- Spider Mites and Aphids

These pests have mouths that suck and pierce through parts of your plants. This can lead to wilting, damaged, or discolored plants. It can also lead to more bugs coming to feed on your plants. For this you will need to apply some sort of spray. You can choose a pesticide or neem oil to spray on the leaves of your plants sparingly.

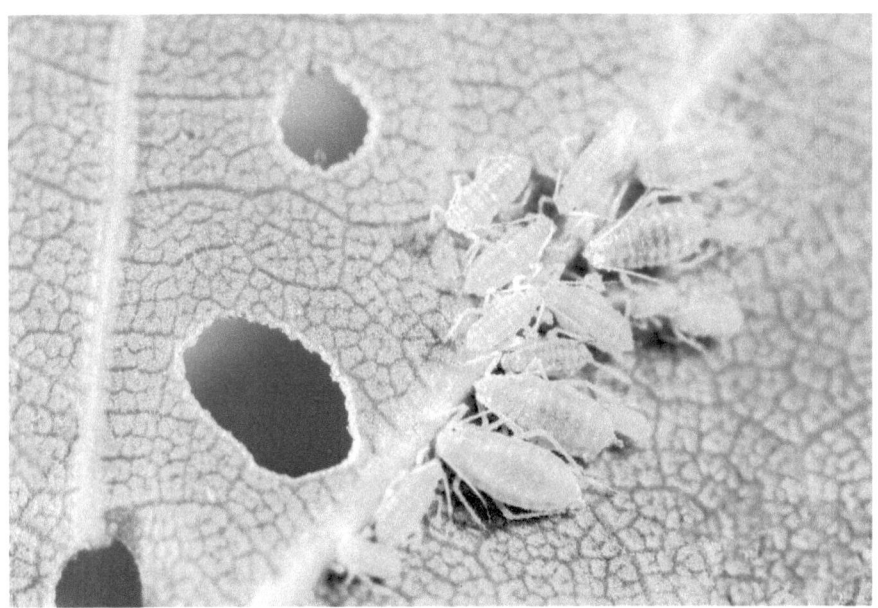

- Silverleaf Whitefly

These pests don't technically eat your plants. Instead, they suck on your plants and leave behind a spit-like substance. This slime can burn through leaves and even attract other pests to the plant due to the sugar in it. You can use insecticides or neem oil to help rid your plants of this pest.

- Cutworms

These bugs come out at night making them the hardest to see and catch. They will eat the leaves and stems of your plants making your plants bare and empty. Since these bugs come out from the ground and soil around your plants you can spray insecticides or neem oil on the base of your plants to help get rid of these pests.

- Powderpost Beetles

These bugs are ones that you have to look out for on your trees and larger plants. Only about ¼ of an inch long, and these beetles will eat your tree trucks from the inside out. If you begin to see the bugs or see small holes in the wood your best bet is to call a professional to get rid of them. The amount of work that is needed to get rid of these bugs may be harmful to you or your plants, so it is best to get professional help.

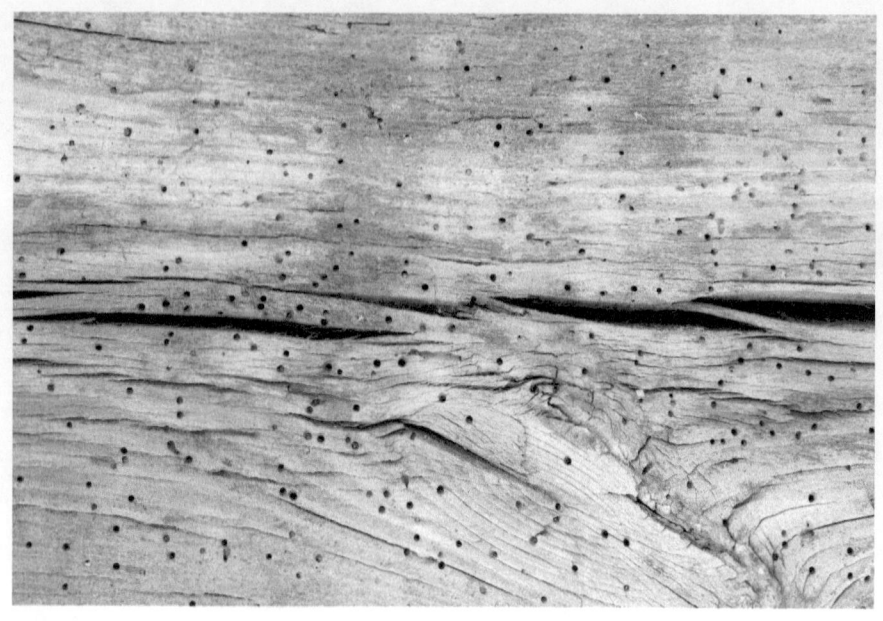

- Blueberry Gall Midge Larvae

These bugs burrow and dig themselves into the leaves and other parts of your plants to help them stay safe until hatching or maturity. This burrowing can lead to inflation of your plant and overall damage. The best way to get rid of these is to spray pesticides. Make sure the one you choose is safe for humans as you don't want to poison your plants.

The Bottom Line

The bottom line here is that when it comes to gardening in Florida, there are some specifications and a little bit more labor involved to make sure your plants thrive. However, despite all of the difficulties, Florida is still one of the most fruitful areas to grow a garden. As long as it is done properly, nearly every fruit and vegetable can be grown within the southern state. It is just up to you to choose which ones you want.

Now that we have gone through the theory, let's get to the practical specifics of growing each individual fruit and vegetable.

Part Two

Fruits

Chapter 3

Apples and Pears

Introduction

For the longest time apples couldn't be grown in Florida. However, you can grow many varieties. Most of the planting instructions for the different varieties are the same. Seek out some of the more resistant and resilient apple trees. They will be easier to care for. Varieties like Breabum, Gala, Anna, Crabapples, and Redprairie Apples.

Another fruit that is rather comparable to the apple is the pear. Only recently have pears been successfully grown in the state of Florida. Again, like the apple, only a select number of species of pears can grow here. For instance, bartletts, hood pears, and pineapple pears have found great success here.

Thankfully, the growing specifications for both apple and pear trees are rather similar. For this reason we have combined their instructions into a single chapter.

Planting

Planting is best from December to February.

Planting Instructions From Seeds or Scraps

Take a cut from an already existing apple tree or pear tree. It should be a small branch or twig that is long enough to stand on its own while still being planted in soil. You want the cutting to be from a healthy tree and not damaged.

Cut the branch of all of its leaves and flowers to make it bare, leave any nodes or buds on the branch. Cut the bottom of the cutting at a 45 degree angle and apply growth and rooting hormone to the end.

Plant the cutting into enriched soil and in a pot. You should never start cutting your apple tree directly from the ground. water to keep the soil moist.

After three to six weeks roots will appear. When the roots are about 1 inch in length, plant in the ground in a full sun area where it can get sunlight for 8 hours per day.

Planting Instructions From A Shrub

Leave the plant outside in your yard for 24-48 hours. Water it well. This will help acclimate the plant to your yard's climate.

Plant in the ground, in a full sun area where it can get sunlight for 8 hours per day.

Planting Companions and Planting Mismatches

Apple Trees

Companions: chamomile, coriander, dill fennel, basil, pear trees

Mismatches: strawberries, chives, peas and beans

Pear Trees

Companions: lavender, clovers, most herbs, apple trees

Mismatches: no known mismatches

Growing and Care

Water daily to keep soil moist. You do not want wet or soaking wet soil: damp soil is fine.

Once you see growth, after 10-14 days, water the plants about 1 inch per week. Do not let the soil dry out, so water more if needed.

As the tree grows, until it becomes a thicker trunk, you may need to attach it to a steak to help support it.

Tips For Pest and Disease Control

Apple and pear trees are notorious for attracting pests and small animals. Thankfully with a little bit of work you can help to deter some of these pests (HGTV).

Prune your apples and pear trees often. By cutting off the dead and diseased leaves, and picking off the rotten apples and pears, will stop most pests from coming to your tree. It will also help disease to stop spreading.

Routinely pick apples and pears that have fallen. Those fruits begin to decompose, releasing their juice and sugars onto the ground. Bugs and small animals will be drawn to this scent and in turn to your tree.

Maggot flies eat and burrow into your apples and pears, running your fruit. You can hang traps for maggot flies in the trees to help attract them away from your fruit.

For Curculio, there are beetles that find their way onto your trees. You can either spray your tree just after it blossoms with a chemical called phosmet- aka Imidan. Or you can cover the base of your tree with a tarp every morning and gently shake your tree until the beetles fall out.

Harvesting

Apples

Apples become heavy and begin to pull away from the branch, as a result they will pull easily out of the branch. The ripe apples will have a firmness to them but they will not be hard. Lastly, most apples with be about the size of a fist or fit into the hand nicely

To harvest the apples you need only to gently pull the apple from the branch. If it requires you to twist or pull hard, the apple is not ready to be picked.

Pears

When it comes to the ripeness of pears you can follow some of the signs as you do with apples. For example the branch will sag and the pair will pull away from the branch as it is heavy with lightness. The pair should be firm and have a little bit of a give to it. It should also fit comfortably in the palm of your hand.

However, there is another way to tell if pears are ready to be harvested. Simply squeeze the stem of the pair. If there is a little bit of give to the stem then the pear is ready to eat. Lastly, the fruit should be released easily from the branch. If you have to tug, pull, or twist it means that the fruit is not ready to be picked.

Once you have determined if your fruit is ripe you need only to protect it from the tree. Be careful not to shake or jostle the tree too much as you could damage potential fruit blooms.

Chapter 4

Avocado

Introduction

There are many varieties of avocados. The most popular Hass avocado does not grow well in Florida, but some varieties do. They include Donnie, Dupuis, and Monroe.

Planting

Planting Instructions From Seeds or Scraps

Harvest your avocado seeds from the fruit. Wash it to remove any excess flesh. Do not remove any of the brown lining and be sure there are no cuts in the pit.

Pay attention to which end was at the bottom of the avocado; this is where the roots will come from. Pierce the pit with three toothpicks so as to support the pit in the glass. Put the root end of the pit in water. Do not let the bottom of the pit touch the bottom of the glass. About half of the avocado should be under the water.

Once you see roots change the water. After about 8 weeks, the top will dry out and crack to aloof for more roots to come. This is called the tap root. Do not let the tap root dry out. You may need to switch to a larger glass to allow this taproot to become longer. Once the root is about 15cm (about 6 inches) long, cut it to about 8 cm (3 inches). Once it grows to about 6 inches a second time you can plant it in soil. Be sure to plant in a pot and leave the top of the pit above the soil.

I live in a very sunny area. Water the plant a lot but don't let the water sit. If the water begins to pool, you've put in too much. Every time your tree grows six inches pinch off the top leaves; this will encourage more growth.

Once you have pinched the leaves three times you can transplant it into the ground. If you do plant on the ground in an area that gets 6 hours of sun per day.

You can also keep it in the pot. and move it to the sun for 6 hrs per day.

Planting Instructions From A Shrub

Leave the plant outside in your yard for 24-48 hours. Water it well. This will help acclimate the plant to your yard's climate.

Plant in the ground, or keep in the pot, in a semi sunny area. Avocados can grow in about 6 hours of sun per day and enjoy shade.

Planting Companions and Planting Mismatches

Companions: lavender, onions, strawberries, basil, garlic

Mismatches: no known mismatches

Growing and Care

If you keep the plant in the pot you can move it around your yard to keep it in the sun for 6 hours a day. Otherwise, make sure your chosen ground spot is appropriate.

Water generously but make sure there is no sitting water. You will also want to be careful of cold weather. Bring your plant inside or cover it if the temperature goes below 75 degrees Fahrenheit (24 Celsius).

Tips For Pest and Disease Control

Avocados are known to be popular with aphids. You can wash your plant with soapy water. A mixture of a single squirt of dishwashing soap, a tsp of neem oil, and water, will do the trick.

Clean and respray every 5 days or as needed: you may need to do this more often if you are continuously getting the bugs.

Harvesting

It is important to know that it can take up to 15 years for an avocado tree to bear fruit, let alone have fruit ready to harvest. Some trees ever bear fruit. Avocados are a very fickle plant.

But for those who do bear fruit, there are a few signs telling you when it is ready to be picked; The branch becomes heavy with the fruit and the fruit turns from bright green to darker green. It releases from the tree easily and it is firm with a little bit of give

Remember that avocados continue to ripen even after being pulled out of the tree. So you can let them ripen on the tree and pull them when needed or you can pull them before they are ripe and let them ripen on the counter. The former option is better for the tree and fruit, but the latter option is better if you are selling or giving away the fruit.

Chapter 5

Bananas

Introduction

There are a number of different species and varieties of bananas that encircle the globe. However, there are only a select few that have found success in the growing conditions of the Florida climate. Some of these species include Namwa, or lady finger bananas, Pisang Raja, Red, and Goldfinger.

Thankfully distinguishing and choosing these different varieties is not that difficult. If you grow your banana from a shrub purchased in Florida then it is likely a variety that will grow in the Florida climate. Likewise, if you grow your bananas from seeds you purchased at a Florida supermarket or greenhouse, you will likely be choosing a variety that is compatible with the climate (Gardening Know How).

Planting

Planting Instructions From Seeds or Scraps

Unfortunately you cannot grow a banana tree from a banana that you have purchased at a local supermarket. On the other hand, you do have an option from growing a banana tree from a seed. The seeds are incredibly difficult to come by. If you want to grow your banana tree from a seed, we highly suggest that you purchase the seeds from a greenhouse and not harvest them yourself.

To grow your banana tree, soak the seeds in room temperature water for 24 to 48 hours. This will help to encourage the seeds to grow.

Plant each seed about 1 inch below the soil surface. Make sure that you plant them about 5 to 6 ft apart because although they are small seeds now they will grow into large trees.

Ensure that the soil stays moist, and that you plant in a full sun area of your yard. In this delicate beginning stage, make sure you avoid the hot, scorching midday sun, so be prepared to shield the seeds from or filter the sunlight.

It can take between three to six months to see your banana plant grow. You might see small Trunks and Stems emerging from the ground but your banana plant won't be established until the three to six-month period is over.

Planting Instructions From A Shrub

Leave the plant outside in your yard for 24-48 hours. Water it well. This will help acclimate the plant to your yard's climate.

Once the shrub has become acclimated to your yard, dig a hole that is twice as wide and twice as deep as the pot your shrub came in. Moisten the soil at the bottom of the hole, place your shrub in it, and cover it with enriched soil.

Water liberally but be careful not to soak the soil. You do not want standing water or puddles in your soil when it comes to growing banana trees.

Planting Companions and Planting Mismatches

Companions: sweet-potatoes, palm trees, hibiscus, ginger and turmeric

Mismatches: no known mismatches

Growing and Care

Banana trees love sunlight and warm temperatures. They also love incredibly moist and enriched soil. This means that you should give your banana plant as much sun as possible while ensuring that the soil stays moist. Soil that is too wet or too dry can harm your banana plant and hinder growth.

Banana trees, until they are fully established, tend to be really delicate therefore in any high winds or incredibly cold temperatures your banana tree should be protected. Moreover, if the sun becomes too hot, filter the sunlight through trees or cover your banana tree in the scorching hours of the day.

The more controlled environment you have for your banana tree the more likely you will have a tree that bears fruit. This is why if you have a warm home you may even want to bring your banana tree indoors.

Tips For Pest and Disease Control

There are a number of pests and diseases that can affect your banana tree. They range from the leaves becoming scales, to being infested at night with emerging pests known as weevils and thrips.

Insecticides are your best bet to counter these pests. They will help to kill infestations as well as deter new infestations from happening. As for the leaves becoming scaly, experts say that including an introduction of ladybugs to your garden can help avoid this disease. The ladybugs will help to eat the dead leaves in addition to eating the insects that lead to scaly leaves.

Harvesting

Your bananas will grow upside down and in bunches. They will be ready to be picked when the flowers at the end of the bananas have fallen off or can be picked easily. Your bananas will look rounded and will be firm. If you are harvesting your bananas for yourself, wait until they begin to change from green to yellow. However, if you are harvesting your bananas in larger batches, harvest them when they are still green and give yourself that extra time to have them ripen off the tree.

The best practice for harvesting your bananas is to cut off the entire bunch and stalk the bananas.

Keep in mind that each banana tree only produces one bunch of bananas. That being said, it can produce up to 240 bananas. But it will only produce that once.

Chapter 6

Blackberries

Introduction

Blackberries are a hardy yet fickle berry to plant in the Florida climate. Keep in mind that if you are planting your berries into the ground you're going to want to plant them between December and February. This will allow your plant to establish itself and bear fruit by the time the spring and summer months come.

Planting

Planting Instructions From Seeds or Scraps

To grow blackberries from scraps you need to take a piece as a branch from a healthy and established blackberry plant. You cannot regrow blackberries from the actual berry.

Once you have your stem from an established plant, cut the bottom of the twig at a 45 degree angle. You will want your stem to be between 4 and 6 in in length and still firm and green inside. You can dip this stem into a rooting hormone to encourage growth, then place the stem in moist peat moss or soil. You will want about two and a half inches of your stem to be below the surface of the soil while the rest of your plant is above. Roots will likely develop between 3 to 4 weeks. For blackberries you do not have to keep them in a bright place. They enjoy the shade with a little bit of sun.

Once these roots begin to develop and you see growth from the top of the cutting, you can transplant your blackberry plant directly into the ground (Growing Blackberries). When you plant your blackberries into the ground, be sure you plant them in a sunny area that is close to a water source. Blackberries love the sun but usually require extra water.

Planting Instructions From A Shrub

Leave the plant outside in your yard for 24-48 hours. Water it well. This will help acclimate the plant to your yard's climate.

Once the plant has gotten used to your yard's climate, dig a hole that is twice as wide and twice as deep as the pot your shrub came in. Moisten the soil at the bottom of the hole, place your shrub in it, and cover it with enriched soil.

Planting Companions and Planting Mismatches

Companions: grapes, mint, raspberries, garlic, apples, chives, strawberries

Mismatches: most peppers, tomatoes, potatoes, eggplants

Growing and Care

Blackberries are relatively low maintenance. They don't require much work as plants themselves to bear fruit. However, you do have to put in a little bit of effort and labor into making sure their environment is perfect. Make sure that the ground is not covered in weeds and that you routinely remove any overgrowth from other plants. Overgrowth can strangle the roots and stems of blackberries, harming berry growth. Additionally, fertilize the ground to make sure there are enough nutrients, but be very careful not to over fertilize the soil for blackberries. Too much fertilizer can burn the delicate leaves of this berry shrub and hinder berry growth.

Other than caring for the environment directly surrounding the blackberry shrub, you only need to make sure the soil stays moist and that the shrub is protected from any extreme weather events.

Tips For Pest and Disease Control

Blackberry plants are incredibly susceptible to aphids, army worms, and cutworms. These will be easy to notice as they usually group together and present themselves as small specks or small worms on the plant.

If you are finding that your blackberry plant is housing this pest, there are a few options to deter them. You can spray your plant with a strong stream of water to help drown and wash away the worms. You can also spray your plant with insecticides. However, since berries don't have protective skin or coating, you have to be incredibly careful with which insecticides you choose. Natural and homemade insecticides tend to be less harmful than those that are commercially produced.

Most importantly, if you do choose to spray insecticide on your blackberry bushes, make sure you wash your blackberries thoroughly before eating them.

Harvesting

Your blackberries will first flower then change color from white to green, to red, and then finally a dark rich bluish black.

You will also be able to tell that your blackberries are ready to be harvested because they release themselves easily from the stems without very much tugging or pulling.

Simply pull the berries off of the branches gently and wash them before eating. Be careful not to shake or jostle the shrub too much when you harvest so as to not damage the other budding and unripened berries.

Chapter 7

Blueberries

Introduction

Only the rabbiteye and the southern highbush variety of blueberries are known to grow well in the Florida climate. Specifically, if you are in the more southern part of the state, choose the southern highbush blueberry. Alternatively, if you are closer to the North, choose the rabbiteye variety.

Thankfully, no matter the variety you choose, you will be able to follow the same growing instructions and specifications.

Planting

Planting Instructions From Seeds or Scraps

Unfortunately, like most berries, you won't be able to grow a blueberry bush from an actual blueberry. However, you will be able to propagate a stem from an already existing and healthy blueberry bush to grow your own.

To do this, simply cut a healthy stem off of a blueberry bush that is about 6 inches long and cut the bottom of the twig at a 45 degree angle.

Feel free to dip this stem into a rooting hormone to encourage growth. You need to then place the stem in moist peat moss or soil. Make sure about two and a half inches of your stem is below the soil while the rest of your plant is above the soil surface. It will take about 3 to 4 weeks for roots to be established. A good sign that the roots are growing and accepting nutrients is that you see growth from the top of your stem.

Once these roots begin to develop and you see growth from the top of the cutting, you can transplant the bush directly into the ground (Growing Blueberries). When you plant your blueberries, make sure you plant them in a sunny area that is close to a water source. You will also want to make sure that you plant your blueberry bush away from any large tree or other kinds of fruits and vegetables that have strong and wandering roots.

Planting Instructions From A Shrub

Leave the plant outside in your yard for 24-48 hours. Water it well. This will help acclimate the plant to your yard's climate.

Once the plant has become familiar with your yard's climate, dig a hole that is twice as wide and twice as deep as the pot your shrub came in. Moisten the soil at the bottom of the hole, place your shrub in it, and cover it with enriched soil.

Although you do not want to plant your blueberries close to any large trees or strong rooted vegetables, you should plant them close to another blueberry bush or their other planting companions. This is because blueberries thrive on cross-pollination and require it to bear fruit continuously.

Planting Companions and Planting Mismatches

Companions: most citrus, most pine trees, strawberries, clover, most herbs

Mismatches: tomatoes

Growing and Care

Blueberries require a lot of nutrients to thrive. This means that they need cross pollination from other plants or they need it in wrist soil. Fertilizers, mulches, and compost can all help to encourage the growth of healthy juicy blueberries. Fertilizers will help enrich the soil and allow the blueberry bush to absorb nutrients, while mulch and compost can help keep the soil moist.

Blueberries love sunlight. However, make sure you water them in the middle of the day so their soil doesn't dry out. We need about 1 inch of water per week while they're being established and about 4 inches of water when you begin to see berries beginning to fruit.

You need to be diligent in making sure there are no weeds or vines that can strangle the roots of your blueberry bush. Moreover, you need to be careful of how popular blueberries are to animals. Birds especially love the sweet and juicy blueberries to feed their babies. Cages and fabric protection can help protect and deter birds from eating blueberries.

Tips For Pest and Disease Control

Similar to blackberries, blueberries are susceptible to aphids and different kinds of worms. However, blueberries also have their own kind of gall wasps and insects that specifically target them.

Thankfully, most of these pests can be removed by a steady and forceful stream of water to wash them away. You can also use insecticides on the plant, however you have to be careful which insecticide you use so as to not harm the berry or to poison it.

Also due to its sweet flavor blueberries tend to attract more aggressive pests like wasps. Be incredibly careful as wasps can become aggressive and sting when provoked.

Harvesting

Blueberries flower and then change from a pale green color into the rich blueberry color they are known for. Once the blueberries are this rich blue color they are ready to be harvested.

Another way of knowing is that the blueberry itself releases easily from the stem. The blueberry should be slightly firm but not hard. You only need to pick the blueberries from the stem and wash them before eating. Just like with every berry bush, make sure you are gentle when you are harvesting your blueberries so as to not harm the unripened berries or the bush itself.

Chapter 8

Citrus

Introduction

The Florida climate is incredibly well known for producing rich, sweet, and juicy citrus fruits. There are a number of different citrus fruits including grapefruits, lemons, limes, and oranges. Each of these fruits also has different species and varieties as well.

Generally speaking, each of these fruit trees follows the same growth and care instructions.

Planting

Planting Instructions From Seeds or Scraps

Perhaps it is annoying but all citrus fruit has seeds, it is from the seeds that you can grow more trees. That being said, growing a citrus tree from a seed can be tedious.

Once you gather the seeds from your chosen citrus fruit you need to test for empty seeds. Put them in a small cup of water. If the seed floats that means there is nothing inside of it that will grow. What you want are the seeds that sink. Next, take a pair of nail clippers and gently remove the gel type coating from the seed, this will help it germinate better. To do this, clip the pointed end of the seed and peel the skin until you are left with the soft inner seed (Will, 2022).

Next you are going to take a handful of sheets of paper towels and spray them with water. Place the individual seeds on a paper towel inches apart from each other. Cover the seeds with another moist paper towel and place the sandwich into a large Tupperware container or plastic bag. Make sure that it is sealed tightly. Place the bag or container in a dark and warm place.

You can check on these seeds every few days to make sure that roots have sprouted. Once there is about an inch's worth of route from the seedlings, you can place each seed into enriched soil. We suggest that you plant the seeds in a pot first to allow the plant to establish itself then transplant the tree into the ground after a few months' time. Place the pot in a sunny and hot area and make sure the soil stays moist.

In about a few weeks you will notice sprouting from the pot. You can either leave the tree in the pot or you can transplant it into the ground. This will of course depend on the citrus you choose as some citrus trees have larger trees than others.

Planting Instructions From A Shrub

Leave the plant outside in your yard for 24-48 hours. Water it well. This will help acclimate the plant to your yard's climate.

Plant in the ground, in a full sun area where it can get sunlight for 8 hours per day. Be sure to dig a hole that is twice as wide and twice as deep as the pot your tree originally came in. This will allow for the routes to establish themselves.

You may also want to think about planting citrus trees beside each other with a couple feet between them. Citrus trees love cross-pollination and will encourage each other to bear fruit.

Planting Companions and Planting Mismatches

Companions: lavender, dill, parsley, thyme, clovers

Mismatches: any plant that is prone to getting mold and mildew

Growing and Care

Citrus trees can be a little sickle to care for. They require full sun but can't be damaged by scorching heat. This means that you should be prepared to protect your citrus trees and incredibly hot weather. Otherwise you only need to water your free when the top inch or two of the soil seems dry when you touch it. When this happens, water generously and then leave the tree alone.

You will also need to prune and trim your tree regularly. Branches and twigs on a citrus tree can grow in unexpected directions and hinder the fruit growth of other healthy branches. Therefore, small branches that are growing in an opposite direction of the rest need to be taken off. Prune small branches from the very top and from the very bottom (*Citrus*).

Tips For Pest and Disease Control

Citrus fruits are sweet and juicy and for that reason attract a variety of pests. Some of these include the citrus Leafminer, the apple moth, and weevils. Unfortunately, many of these pests will require professional removal. Or if not for professional removal they will need insecticides to help deter them.

Some insecticides can be toxic to the fruit. For this reason, it is highly suggested that you opt for more natural insecticide and repellent. For instance, repellents based with garlic can help make the sweet smelling fruit less attractive to the insects (*Citrus Pests*).

Harvesting

Fruits will always bloom as a flower first and then produce the actual food. Citrus trees are no stranger or exception to this rule. Healthy and vibrant balloons are a good sign that juicy and bountiful citrus will follow. Try not to touch or mess with the flowers too much as it can hinder the citrus growth.

Your citrus will be ready when the flour is easily removed or has completely fallen off. Green leaves will likely be attached to the stem of your citrus fruit and the branch holding the fruit will wilt a little bit due to the heft of the food. Your fruit should be vibrant in its assigned color and should be firm but have a little bit of a give to it: it should not be hard nor should it be completely squishy. Hardness is a sign that it is not ready and two soft means that it is past its prime and can be perhaps rotten.

Gently pull the fruit from the branch. If it is right it should be released easily. Be gentle when you pull the fruit off the tree so as to not damage the other unripened fruit or flowers.

Chapter 9

Grapes

Introduction

The sheer amount of different kinds of grapes there are in the world is overwhelming. That being said, three specific types of grapes have shown great success to be grown in the Florida climate. They are the muscadine grape, bunch grapes, and a combination and hybrid of these two kinds.

Still, growing grapes takes an incredible amount of patience and care when growing them in Florida. In fact, some experts say that it's best to avoid growing grapes in Florida because it is near impossible. While it is difficult it is not impossible and if you grow grapes successfully you will be given a sense of accomplishment that you will never be able to reach otherwise.

Planting

Planting Instructions From Seeds or Scraps

Because grapes are so difficult to grow in the Florida climate, we strongly suggest that you do not grow grapes from cuttings, scraps, or seeds. Doing so will give you a higher chance of failure, will bring about more frustration, and will ultimately lead to waste of time.

This of course is not meant to be discouraging, we simply want to provide you with the best way possible to grow your grapes. In this case, grow grapes from a shrub.

Planting Instructions From A Shrub

The reason why you should grow grapes purchased at a greenhouse is that they are suited to the climate and are able to grow. There is less of a chance of you choosing the wrong variety of grapes. On the other hand, much of the hard propagating and growing work has already been done for you. When growing grapes, failure and trouble happens in the early stages of sprouting. If you purchase a previously established shrub all of that work has been done for you and you are on a better road towards success.

Once you have purchased your grapes, leave the plant outside in your yard for 24-48 hours. Water it well. This will help acclimate the plant to your yard's climate. Once the grapevine has become acclimated to your yard, dig a hole that is twice as wide and twice as deep as the pot your shrub came in. Moisten the soil at the bottom of the hole, place your shrub in it, and cover it with enriched soil.

Water liberally but be careful not to soak the soil. You do not want standing water or puddles in your soil when it comes to growing grapes. (*Grapes to grow in Florida*)

Planting Companions and Planting Mismatches

Companions: elm trees, basil, most beans, oregano, peas

Mismatches: garlic

Growing and Care

Plant your grapes in an area that gets full sun during the day, but also has a little bit of shade to shield the delicate grapes from the extreme weather that can happen in Florida. Grapevines can survive in areas with heavy rain and with drought or dry periods.

If you notice the top two inches of your soil drying out, make sure that the soil beneath stays moist. If you find the soil continues to dry out, feel free to liberally water the grapes. If you go through a period of time where there is heavy rainfall, you should check the soil before watering so as to not over water the plant.

You will want to make sure you prune away any rogue branches or branches that are growing against healthy ones. You should also remove branches at the bottom.

You will also want to fertilize your grapes. Fertilizers such as bone meals or natural homemade fertilizers do best. When your grape vines first begin to brand out, apply about a quarter of a pound of fertilizer regularly. Then as your grapes become more mature, fertilize more often and increase the poundage to 2 to 3 lbs.

Tips For Pest and Disease Control

Grapes attract pests, such as weevils and grape mites. These pests will eat the leaves and the fruits of the vines, and even bury themselves into the stems and trunks. As a result they can compromise an entire Grapevine.

You can professionally remove these pests, however natural insecticides are highly suggested. Due to the delicate nature of the grape you do not want to be spraying chemical insecticides, pesticides, or herbicides on your plants.

You may also want to opt for stinky, homemade insecticides to help counteract the grapes' sweet smell.

Harvesting

Grapes will grow on a branch. They will have a stem and that stem will hold a bunch or a handful of grapes. You will notice that your grapes are ready to harvest when they are slightly firm but have a little bit of a gift to them. They should not be hard nor should they be squishy. The branch housing them may even sag a little bit on the vine showing that the grapes are full of juice.

To harvest the grapes you do not want to pick each individual grape off of the bunch. Rather you can take a pair of sharp garden shears or scissors and cut the bunch of grapes off of the branch. Keeping the stem of the bunch intact as much as possible will help keep your grapes healthy.

The stem of the bunch won't be removed easily but it should not be difficult to cut. If the stem is not cut nicely it could mean that the grapes are not yet fully ripe.

Chapter 10

Mango

Introduction

Mangoes love warmer climates, which is why they grow well in Florida. That being said, there can be some difficulties growing this route which means a little bit of due diligence needs to be taken and some careful oversight.

However, if done properly, you will be producing juicy ripe mangoes on a consistent basis.

Planting

Planting Instructions From Seeds or Scraps

Growing mangoes from seeds is one of the more popular ways of growing this fruit. This is because the pit and seed, after being handled and propagated properly, will usually yield a healthy mango tree. First you want to remove the husky and pit out of the mango. Make sure the mango you're using is ripe and healthy. If not, the pit will likely be unhealthy as well.

Wash the husk thoroughly and dry it entirely. As you scrub and wash you will notice that the husk begins to get a little bit hairy or stringy. Using a knife you can gently cut off all of these strings or hairs. Once the husk has dried completely, using a sharp pair of scissors, cut up the seams of the husk. Pry it open and pull out the seed itself. It will look like a giant bean.

Take a paper towel and make it damp and wet by spraying it with water. Wrap it around the seed and put the package in a plastic bag. Next, put the bag in a dark place. A cupboard or drawer will do just fine. Check back on the seed every few days, but don't wait longer than three days at a time. You might miss an important step otherwise.

Once you notice that the seed is rooting, wait until the route is about 3 inches long. Once it reaches that point you can plant your seed into a pot with enriched soil. Place the seed flat on the soil with the root facing up. Gently cover your seed with soil and water it thoroughly.

Place your pot in a very sunny and warm location but be wary of direct heat and sunlight. If you are putting it outside, the plant should be protected or have filtered sun. Do it in the morning, late afternoon, and evening. It will take a while for your mango plant to be healthy and large enough to be planted outside. Until then, allow for the plants to grow and bloom indoors or in your pot. As it grows, transfer it to a larger pot. Be patient and hold off from planting it in the ground right away (Will, 2021).

Planting Instructions From A Shrub

Leave the plant outside in your yard for 24-48 hours. Water it well. This will help acclimate the plant to your yard's climate.

After about two days, dig a hole in the ground twice as deep and twice as wide as the pot the shrub originally came in. Cover with rich soil and water thoroughly. Follow the same planting in sunlight instructions as above. You should know that it is totally okay to leave your mango plant in the pot it came in for at least a little while. Once you notice that it starts becoming larger and over growing the pot you can transplant it then.

Planting Companions and Planting Mismatches

Companions: Any citrus tree

Mismatches: A mango tree can grow in its pot for its entire life. Mangoes don't necessarily have mismatches or poor growing companions.

Growing and Care

Mango trees are incredibly durable and resilient. As long as you follow their sun and water needs you will likely see fruit in a few years from growing. As mentioned above, mangoes love hot sun but are susceptible to burning and wilting in scorching heat. Build a pergola or plant your mango tree where sunlight can be filtered through other trees. You can also keep it in its own pot and move the plant around your yard according to weather and sun conditions.

As for watering, mangoes can be easily over-watered. Wait until at least the top 3 inches of soil is dry to the touch in the bottom soil is moist. At that point generously water your tree. Once you notice that blooms begin to come out, pull back on the water and just a little bit, and begin regular watering again once you notice the blooms are turning into fruits.

Tips For Pest and Disease Control

Mango trees are susceptible to many of the same pests that citrus trees are susceptible to. This means that the ways to rid your mango trees of the pests are the same as well.

Strong streams of water to drown and wash away the bugs will work well. Spraying the tree with insecticides will help as well. Due to the mango's hardy exterior, you have a little more freedom in the insecticide you choose. Be careful not to over spray as it can still be harmful to the fruit.

More dangerous than pests is the cold for mango trees. Be very careful of frost, cold rain, and chilling winds. This will damage the fruit on your tree and the tree itself.

Harvesting

Mangoes are ripe when they have a mixture between a green yellow and red color. The more red the mango is, the riper it is. It should be firm but have a little bit of a gift to it. Hard mangoes are not right, and mushy mangoes are too ripe.

Notice the branch with the heft and weight of the right mango. All you need to do is gently pull the fruit off of the branch. If the fruit doesn't release itself easily, it is not right. Careful not to jostle or shake the tree too much, as you could damage the other fruit and branches.

Chapter 11

Melons

Introduction

Melons cover a range of different fruits. Usually they grow on vines and along the ground and produce food with a hard rind and juicy fruit inside. Three of the more commonly known melons are watermelon, cantaloupes, and honeydew.

The key when planting multiple kinds of melons in your yard is to plant them far away from each other. Other than that, they can grow relatively under the same circumstances. For this reason we have grouped them together as one kind of fruit to grow.

Planting

Planting Instructions From Seeds or Scraps

Melons have their seeds inside of them. In fact, you usually scrape them out before you eat the fruit. You can plant these seeds to grow more melons. However, due to Florida's unpredictable climate, we suggest that you find melon plants that have already sprouted.

Growing full melons from seeds takes quite a long time and a lot can go wrong during that time period. Specifically, melons are incredibly susceptible to cold weather. Therefore, planting a seed requires more specific planning than planting an already established plant.

Planting Instructions From A Shrub

Instead we suggest going to a greenhouse or a garden center and purchasing already sprouted melon plants. This way you know the seed is viable and you are more likely to have success. Once you purchase your melon plant, leave the plant outside in your yard for 24-48 hours. Water it well. This will help acclimate the plant to your yard's climate.

After the two-day waiting period, dig a hole twice as wide and twice as deep as the pot it came in. Melons have deep roots and will need room to grow.

Plant your melon in a full sun area about 2 to 4 ft apart from anything else - even companion planting. Make sure you plant in the warmer months of the year. You may even want to use heating mats to warm the soil before you plant.

During this establishment, make sure the soil stays moist. Dry soil is deadly for melons. Once you see significant growth of your fruit, then you can rely on rainfall or a scheduled watering pattern.

Planting Companions and Planting Mismatches

Cantaloupes

Companions: Marigolds, most lettuce varieties, radishes

Mismatches: cucumbers, watermelons, most gourds and squash varieties

Honey Dew

Companions: Basil, Broccoli, most corn, mint, dill

Mismatches: Cucumber and watermelon

Water Melon

Companions: Dill, most annual flowers like marigold, chamomile

Mismatches: most squash varieties, most potatoes, cucumbers, other melons

Growing and Care

When you have an established melon plant, water them infrequently. But when you water them you want to fully saturate the soil. For example, you want to fully saturate 2 inches of soil once a week or every two weeks depending on how dry the soil gets. When you notice that the fruits are beginning to ripen, cut back on the watering to allow the fruit to mature.

Another way to carefully care for your melon plants is to weed the area frequently. Vines tend to grow and weave their way around. Weeds can strangle the vine or even stop melon growth. Be careful not to use pesticides or any weed killer because the melon roots will absorb the chemicals and make the melons dangerous to eat.

Tips For Pest and Disease Control

Melons are special because not only do they attract aphids and mites, they specifically attract melon aphids and melon spider mites. This just means that they are a specific species of insect that is nearly always found by your melons.

Your best bet to get rid of these aphids and other pests, luckily, is to follow the same instructions we've mentioned throughout. Spray your melons with a powerful stream of water to drown and wash away the insects. You can also spray your melons with different insecticides to help deter their return. Since melons have a hard and thick rind surrounding the fruit inside, you show a little bit more freedom with the insecticide you choose. You can also spray them a little bit more liberally since there is less of a chance of the insecticide leaching into the fruit. That being said, you should still be careful not to over spray, and you should always opt for more natural or homemade insecticides.

Harvesting

Signs of Ripeness for Cantaloupes

There are a few key signs to know when cantaloupes are ready to be picked. In fact, in most cases they will detach themselves from the main Vine. However, if you want to know when your cantaloupes are ready before they fall off you will be able to smell it. they will smell musky yet sweet when ripe. their rind will be textured with white bumps and yellowish green skin.

Signs of Ripeness for Honey Dew

To know that your honeydew is ready to be harvested you should look at the rind first and foremost. The rind of the honey dew will be smooth and even in color. It will feel firm and a little waxy. You should also hear a hollow sound when you tap on the melon. Some experts say that if you press on the bottom edge of the melon - the part that is not attached to the main vine, and it has a little bit of a give to it, then the melon is ripe. Simply cut it from the main vine. Be careful not to damage the main vine when harvesting the melon (Gardeners).

Signs of Ripeness for Watermelon

Some signs of ripeness for watermelon are that they are heavy, smell sweet, sound hollow when knocked on, and there is usually a yellowish spot on the underside or bottom of the melon. You can also tell by it having a nice consistent webbing pattern around it and it has a tightly curled vine coming out of the vine. To harvest, you only need to cut or pick the watermelon from the vine. Try not to cut the main vine of the watermelon, as it can damage it and hurt the growth of other melons (Master Class).

Chapter 12

Papaya

Introduction

Papayas are a large squash shaped fruit that has the same color as mangoes. For this reason they are oftentimes considered to be in the same fruit family. This is, unfortunately, a misnomer. Papayas have a sweet flavor but tend to not smell the greatest; and are totally different from mangoes.

That being said, they have been found to have much success growing in the state of Florida; this is perhaps the strongest similarity between them and mangoes.

Planting

Planting Instructions From Seeds or Scraps

When you cut open a papaya you will find a plethora of small black seeds. These can be used to grow your papaya from. However, we do not recommend it. The seeds of a papaya require some careful handling and are temperamental when it comes to regrowth.

If you have the temperature controls of an established greenhouse, then growing this tropical fruit from seeds is very forgiving. However, if you are growing the plant in your backyard, then purchase an established plant (VanZile, 2022).

Planting Instructions From A Shrub

After you have chosen your papaya plant, leave the plant outside in your yard for 24-48 hours. Water it well. This will help acclimate the plant to your yard's climate.

After this two day period you have two choices. You can transplant it into the ground or you can move it to a larger pot. For this fruit, transplant it to another pot to give it more room to grow both upwards and through the roots. A pot about 18 inches in diameter and that holds 15-20 gallons should be big enough.

If you plant into the ground, dig a hole that is twice as big and twice as deep as the pot that you got the fruit in.

No matter what, your papaya plant should be put in a place that gets eight hours of sunlight per day. Make sure you shelter the plant from cold snaps and winds, while also keeping the soil moist.

Once you see significant growth or flowers start to bud then you can continue to water on its own watering schedule.

Planting Companions and Planting Mismatches

Companions: Beans, most annual flowers, bananas, and sweet potatoes

Mismatches: No significant mis-matches

Growing and Care

Papayas need quite a bit of heat to bear fruit successfully. This means that you may need to bring in the plant during the colder months or cover the plant if it is planted into the ground.

You should water the plant every 3-4 days. Do not let the soil dry out. Papayas need lots of water to grow. Do not let water sit on top of the soil. If you see small puddles forming, then stop watering.

You will also want and need to prune your papaya plant often. When it comes to fruit trees, twigs and branches can grow against each other and in all kinds of directions. You should cut those smaller or damaged branches so they do not harm the healthy ones. You will also want to remove the ones that are at the bottom of the tree, and those that shoot out beyond others. This will give the fruit places to grow while also encouraging new fruit to grow after harvest.

Tips For Pest and Disease Control

Papayas have a woodier kind of trunk. This means that they are susceptible to root rot. This happens because people tend to over water their papaya plants since they love water so much. To rectify this, make sure that you have soil that drains well. This will help stop water from sitting in the soil without being absorbed into the plants.

You also need to be careful of rainfall. If you have heavy rainfall, or rainfall of any kind, make sure you test the soil before going out to water your papaya tree. If the top of the soil looks and feels dry then you can feel free to water it until the top soil looks and feels wet. If the ground still looks damp, hold off on watering. You can also use fertilizers and compost to help your soil stay moist and encourage nutrient absorption by the plant, which will help alleviate the pressure of over watering the fruit.

Harvesting

After about 6-12 months, your fruits will be ready for harvest. The papayas will turn from green to a bright yellow and the branches will sag slightly. They will also be easily removed from their respective branches. If you have to tug, twist, or pull the fruit off then it wasn't as ripe as you may have thought.

To harvest you only need to reach up and pick the fruit directly off of the tree.

Chapter 13

Peaches, Plums, Nectarines, and Other Stone Fruits

Introduction

Stone fruits are those round fruits that, at their center, sit in a singular hard pit. This pit is where the fruits get their name as 'stone fruits'. There are many varieties and species of stone fruits that are available to you but the three that are most popular are peaches, plums, and nectarines.

Thankfully each stone fruit grows under similar conditions. This means if you can grow one you can likely grow all of them. You need to choose, however, the specific kinds of stone fruit you want. Each has its own flavor, texture, and look to them. After your selection the rest is rather simple.

Planting

Planting Instructions From Seeds or Scraps

Choose a healthy stone fruit of whatever kind and variety that you like. Remove all of the skin and flesh surrounding the pit. Wash all the flesh out of the pit and allow the pit to dry for up to a month before placing it in any sort of growing conditions.

Using a hammer, hit and smash the pit open. It will provide you with small seeds that almost look like almonds. Once you've acquired these almond-shaped seeds, fill a jar with some enriched potting soil and add just enough water to moisten it. Add the individual seeds to the jar and give it a little shake to encourage the seeds to be enveloped by the soil. Leave the jar in the fridge.

This can take up to four months. You may notice that roots start coming out of the seeds. This is a sign that they are ready to be planted.

In small individual pots, add enough soil to fill it to about 1/3. Gently place your seed with the root on top of the soil, and then cover with about an inch of soil. Water the seeds well and leave them outside in the bright sun. Make sure you keep the soil damp and after about two weeks you will likely see green leaves and stems sprouting from the soil. Feel free to place a steak in the pot to encourage the stem and tree to grow until it is fully established.

Once you see significant growth, and your tree begins to be too large for the small pot, you can transplant it into a larger pot or directly into the ground. Still keep the tree in a sunny and warm area while keeping the soil moist (Levin).

Planting Instructions From A Shrub

Once you choose the stone fruit variety that you want, leave the plant outside in your yard for 24-48 hours. Water it well. This will help acclimate the plant to your yard's climate.

Leave the plant outside in your yard for 24-48 hours. Water it well. This will help acclimate the plant to your yard's climate.

Once the plant has gotten used to your yard's climate, dig a hole that is twice as wide and twice as deep as the pot your shrub came in. Moisten the soil at the bottom of the hole, place your shrub in it, and cover it with enriched soil.

Planting Companions and Planting Mismatches

Companions: basil, most onions, garlic

Mismatches: Grasses, most potatoes, tomatoes, Raspberries

Growing and Care

The best way to care for your stone fruit trees is to do so through a calendar. If we begin with March or late winter, it is important that you prune your trees. Plant your new stone fruit trees in the spring and early summer. Then from the summer into the early fall is my new all likely Harvest. Then, from the middle of fall to winter, do some winterizing. If you choose to plant your stone fruit tree on the ground this could mean rapping it for the winter months; whereas if you keep it in a pot this can mean bringing it indoors.

Generally you want to make sure that your stone fruit tree gets plenty of sun and you water it correctly.

Tips For Pest and Disease Control

Stone fruit trees, due to the sweet and juicy nature of their fruit, attract many of the same insects as citrus and apple trees do. However, you can easily rid your stone fruit tree of the small pests through the same methods you would for citrus are apple trees.

What you should be more concerned about with these trees are the small animals that will be attracted to them. Birds and small rodents, we'll pluck your stone fruit directly out of the tree and take it for themselves.

Unfortunately the only way to keep small animals away from your stone fruit tree is to keep them indoors entirely. However, if you are keeping your trees outside, you've been surrounded by cages or put other sorts of deterrence around your tree. Just be careful that your deterrent isn't harming the tree or the humans tending to the tree. One big deterrent is to make sure the bottom of your tree is clean. Remove any fallen branches or fruits that are rotting on the ground. As these fruits decompose they release a sweet smell into the air which attracts the small animals. Picking these fruits out before they decompose can help to deter animals from being attracted to your fruit. You can also use insecticides that have poor smells to them. The poor smell can mask the sweet smell of the fruit.

Harvesting

Stone fruits are considered ripe when they fit comfortably in the palm of your hand. Of course if you choose a plum or a cherry these fruits will be much smaller. To truly test the ripeness, give the fruit a light and gentle squeeze. The food should be firm but have a little bit of a gift to it. If your fingers go right through the fruit then it is overripe, however if it feels hard like a baseball then it is not ripe yet.

The tree itself will give you signs that the fruit it bares is ripe and ready to be picked. Branches will sag slightly and the fruit will be released from the branch quite easily with just a gentle tug (Hoover).

To harvest the stone fruit you need only to pick it with your hand off of the tree. Be very careful. Stone fruits like peaches are prone to bruising very easily. On the other hand, you do not want to shake or jostle the branch too much as it can harm the unripened or budding fruit. A good rule of thumb is if the fruit doesn't come off right away don't force it. You can always go back the next day to check its ripeness once more.

Chapter 14

Persimmon

Introduction

Persimmons look like orange or yellow tomatoes. They have a similar taste and texture yet are slightly more sour and bitter than your average tomato. Due to these similarities in taste, texture, and looks many people believe that persimmons are part of the tomato family. This is incorrect. Persimmons are closer to berries than tomatoes.

No matter their familial connection, persimmons are an interesting fruit to grow and that will add quite a bit of color and variety to your backyard garden.

Planting

Planting Instructions From Seeds or Scraps

Unfortunately it is now impossible to grow a persimmon from its scraps in Florida. The Florida climate is rather temperamental and will likely be damaging to the delicate scraps of the persimmon. On the same note, growing a persimmon tree from seeds in the Florida climate is just as improbable.

Where some fruits and vegetables are able to be successfully grown from their seeds or scraps, persimmons are not one of them. Instead, we highly suggest that you grow your persimmons from an already established plant. You will have much more success and much less of a headache in your growing procedures. individuals who have access to commercial farms and greenhouses will be more successful in growing persimmons from seeds. However, because we are talking about fruits and vegetables that can be grown in the home or in the backyard, persimmons need a little bit of a head start.

However, this doesn't mean that you have to purchase an individual plant. Some individuals who have more advanced backyard gardens have shown great success in growing persimmons from cuttings of other established persimmon trees.

Your cutting should be a small branch or twig that is long enough to stand on its own while still being planted in soil. You want the cutting to be from a healthy tree and not damaged.

Cut the branch of all of its leaves and flowers to make it bare, leave any nodes or buds on the branch. Cut the bottom of the cutting at a 45 degree angle and apply growth and rooting hormone to the end.

Plant the cutting into enriched soil and in a pot. You should never start your persimmon tree cutting directly in the ground. Water it to keep the soil moist.

When the roots begin to grow and are about 1 inch in length, plant in the ground in a full sun area where it can get sunlight for 8 hours per day.

Planting Instructions From A Shrub

Another option for growing Persimmons is to grow from a shrub purchased from a greenhouse or garden center.

Leave your persimmon plant outside in your yard for 24-48 hours. Water it well. This will help acclimate the plant to your yard's climate. After this acclimation period, dig a hole twice as deep and twice as wide as the pot you got it in. Persimmons need to be planted deep into the ground, and this size hole will be sufficient.

You should choose a sunny spot as much as you can, however Persimmons are able to tolerate some shade. Keep the soil moist but not soaking wet. Just like other trees, persimmon trees dislike standing water in their soil. Once you see significant growth, you can water it.

Planting Companions and Planting Mismatches

Companions: mint, chives, most annuals

Mismatches: walnut trees

Growing and Care

Since it is a tree it needs to be pruned. This means that you need to remove any extra twigs and branches. Cut off any that are growing between blooms, or that are growing in the way of other healthier branches. Branches on the bottom part of the tree should be pruned regularly as well as those that reach beyond the top of the tree.

Other than pruning, the only important note to caring for persimmons is to keep them well watered. They do not do well in times of drought or very hot climates. However, general rainfall should be enough to keep the plant happy. Just keep your eyes on the top of the soil. Do not let the first two inches dry out.

Tips For Pest and Disease Control

Persimmon trees are susceptible to scales on their leaves in addition to fruit flies and other insects and animals that are drought to its sweet tart taste. You can wash away these insects with a heavy stream of water. You may also want to spray your tree with insecticide - perhaps one that smells bad - to help mask the smell of the fruit.

You will also want to remove the leaves that have become scaled so they do not infect others around it.

Harvesting

You will know that your persimmons are ripe when they are firm but have a little bit to give to them. They should feel like a firm tomato in your hand. Any harder means they are not ripe, any softer means they are too ripe. You will also know by color. Depending on the variety the color of a ripe persimmon will be an even orange or yellow color. This differs from the bright green they start out as.

Like other tree fruits you will be able to tell that the fruit is ripe based on the tree itself. The branches will sag slightly from the weight of the fruit, and will allow the fruit to be released easily.

For ripe persimmons you would just need to reach out and pick them with your hands.

Chapter 15

Raspberries

Introduction

Raspberries are another berry that can be successfully grown in Florida. Because they are sun and water loving, they can be a little tricky to keep balanced, however with careful planting you can have raspberries year round.

Planting

Planting Instructions From Seeds or Scraps

To grow raspberries from scraps you need to take a piece as a branch from a healthy and established blackberry plant. Unfortunately, you cannot regrow raspberries from the actual fruit

Once you have your stem from a plant, cut the bottom of it at a 45 degree angle. Your stem should be between 4 and 6 in in length and still firm and green inside. You can dip this stem into a rooting hormone to encourage growth, then place the stem in moist peat moss or soil. Make sure that two and a half inches of your stem is below the surface of the soil while the rest of your plant is above. Roots will likely develop between 3 to 4 weeks.

Once these roots begin to develop and you see growth from the top of the cutting, you can transplant your blackberry plant directly into the ground. When you plant your raspberries into the ground, be sure you plant them in a sunny area that is close to a water source. Raspberries love the sun but usually require extra water.

Planting Instructions From A Shrub

Leave the plant outside in your yard for 24-48 hours. Water it well. This will help acclimate the plant to your yard's climate.

Once the plant has gotten used to your yard's climate, dig a hole that is twice as wide and twice as deep as the pot your shrub came in. Moisten the soil at the bottom of the hole, place your shrub in it, and cover it with enriched soil.

Planting Companions and Planting Mismatches

Companions: raspberries spread far so they shouldn't be planted too close to anything except other raspberry plants.

Mismatches: potatoes, beets, and other berries that have just been planted

Growing and Care

Raspberries love sunlight. Therefore, they should be planted in an area that gets 6-8 hours of direct sunlight a day.

Make sure that you water your bush regularly and don't let the soil dry out too much. Raspberry bushes are rather hardy however you want to make sure there are no vines or roots from other plants intruding in the way of the raspberry bush. In fact, plan multiple raspberry bushes within a few feet of each other instead. Raspberries love cross-pollination and encourage each other to grow.

Tips For Pest and Disease Control

Similar to blackberries and blueberries, raspberries are susceptible to aphids and different kinds of worms. However, they also have their own kind of sawfly and pests.

Thankfully, most of these pests can be removed by a steady and forceful stream of water to wash them away. You can also use insecticides on the plant, however you have to be careful which insecticide you use so as to not harm the berry or to poison it.

Also due to its sweet flavor these berries tend to attract more aggressive pests like wasps. Be incredibly careful as wasps can become aggressive and sting when provoked.

Harvesting

Raspberries begin with blooming flowers, turn a pale white green color, then turn to the deep red we know them for. When they become this deep red they are ready to be picked. Carefully pull each raspberry out of the bush. Watch out for the thorns in the bush.

Chapter 16

Strawberries

Introduction

Strawberries are, arguably, one of the most popular fruits in the world, let alone a popular berry. Their versatility and flavor make them a staple in every fridge. Growing strawberries in the state of Florida means that some changes need to be made to the growing instructions to make sure your strawberry plant is fruitful.

Planting

Planting Instructions From Seeds or Scraps

It is possible to grow strawberries from seeds and from scraps. However, even in the most compatible growing environment it is incredibly difficult to successfully regrow strawberries from scraps. On the other hand, growing from seeds takes time and effort, and even then some strawberry seeds don't sprout.

We highly suggest that you do not choose to grow your strawberries from scraps or seeds. There are just too many variables within the Florida climate that will make growing your own strawberry plant from cuttings or seeds incredibly difficult. Larger and more experienced farmers will be able to grow such a plant more easily because they have more control over the environmental elements. However, in your backyard you may not have such control. It is much better for the success of your plant to grow from a shrub purchased from a greenhouse or garden center.

Planting Instructions From A Shrub

Once you have selected your strawberry plant, leave the plant outside in your yard for 24-48 hours. Water it well. This will help acclimate the plant to your yard's climate.

Feel free to leave the strawberry bush in the pot that you purchased it in. But you can also plant it in the ground or a raised garden bed. If you choose to transplant, however, be sure to dig a hole twice as deep and twice as wide as the pot you were given. This will allow for more room for the roots to grow.

Place or plant your strawberries in full sun but be wary of scorching weather. Strawberries love sunlight but are susceptible to burning and rot and incredibly hot sun. If you have your strawberry plant in a pot you can bring it indoors during the hotter hours of the day or you can move it around your house to find filtered sunlight or shade. If your strawberry plant is on the ground, consider a removable pergola or other partially shaded cover to filter sunlight and protect your strawberries during midday.

Planting Companions and Planting Mismatches

Companions: beans, garlic, lettuce, onions, most peas, spinach, thyme

Mismatches: Fennel

Growing and Care

Caring for your strawberry plant is arguably simple. Make sure the soil doesn't get too dry or too wet: make sure that the sun isn't too damaging yet that the plant is getting enough sunlight. Strawberries are the epitome of a balancing act.

Rid the ground of any weeds or encroaching plants to help encourage the growth of the strawberries. Plant your strawberries close to one of its planting companions. Like other berries, strawberries thrive on cross pollination and enjoy being planted beside certain other foods.

Tips For Pest and Disease Control

Strawberries, like every other berry, are prone to attracting aphids and other kinds of worm insects. Likewise due to their sweet taste they can attract small animals and bees. To deter smaller animals you can put up fences or cages around the strawberry plant. However, for the smaller insects you can follow some of the other procedures we've mentioned above, like a steady stream of forceful water to wash them away or spraying insecticides.

However, because the berry is eaten altogether and there is no protective skin, be very selective with the insecticides that you choose. You also need to be careful when you are dealing with bees or wasps that can be drawn to strawberries. These can be incredibly harmful and dangerous to humans as they sting when provoked.

Harvesting

Strawberries Bloom beautiful white flowers before growing green strawberries. These green strawberries turn into a pale white or cream color before they turn into a deep red.

Once the strawberries are red and larger they're ready to be picked. You may notice some of the strawberry branches sag or droop a little bit if the branch that is holding ripe strawberries because of their heft. Strawberries should be easily released from their branches when they are picked. If you have to tug, pull or twist the strawberry off of the shrub then it may not be ripe.

Some varieties of strawberries don't become this deep red, but rather stay white or become a pale pink. Pay attention to which variety you get so you know what color strawberries should be when ripe.

Part Three

Vegetables

Chapter 17

Broccoli

Introduction

For many broccoli seems to be forgotten when it comes to a plant that is grown. In fact many individuals who do not garden broccoli themselves have no idea how it grows and what it looks like when it grows. Broccoli grown in your own garden can taste sweeter and be much healthier for you than its supermarket counterparts.

This is because you can control the pesticides and chemicals used to encourage growth and you can harvest the broccoli at its peak ripeness, instead of relying on the ripeness of the broccoli at the store.

Planting

Planting Instructions From Seeds or Scraps

Although it is possible for you to regrow broccoli from scratch or from seeds, we suggest that, if you are growing in the state of Florida, you don't. Growing broccoli from scraps is an unreliable way of yielding a bountiful harvest. This is because sometimes the roots don't grow properly or they fail to establish themselves. On the other hand, choosing to grow broccoli from seeds takes quite a long time.

To save you quite a bit of time and headaches, we suggest that you grow your broccoli from an already established shrub.

Planting Instructions From A Shrub

After you purchase your broccoli shrug from your house greenhouse or garden center, leave the plant outside in your yard for 24-48 hours. Water it well. This will help acclimate the plant to your yard's climate.

After this 48 hour period, you can transplant your broccoli shrub into either a larger pot or into the ground. If you choose to transplant it to a pot, make sure that it can hold about 5 gallons or more. If you are transplanting into the ground, dig a hole that is twice as deep and twice as wide as the pot. This extra space in the ground and in the pot will allow the roots to grow and establish themselves in a healthy way.

Planting Companions and Planting Mismatches

Companions: Celery, Dill, Rosemary

Mismatches: Strawberries, Tomatoes, Oregano

Growing and Care

Generally speaking, broccoli enjoys hot weather and warm sun. Therefore, you should plant or place your broccoli in an area where it gets direct warm sun for about six hours a day. When your broccoli plant is first being established, and when you notice broccoli florets growing, be very careful of hot scorching midday sun. This can burn a young plant and damage the mature florets. You may also want to consider some sort of filtered sunlight or temporary shade option for your broccoli. In the colder months, allowing your broccoli to have some shade will help prevent it bolting and flowering, rendering the broccoli inedible and elongating its ripeness lifespan.

Broccoli needs to be watered frequently. They are incredibly susceptible to overwatering. However, when the soil becomes dry you need to liberally and deeply water it. This means you can wait for the first inch of soil to become dry before you water it: but when you do water it makes sure the water reaches the roots all the way to the soil surface.

Unbeknownst to most, broccoli grows with quite a bit of foliage and leaves around it. These leaves are meant to protect it from insects, small animals, and environmental elements. However, sometimes these leaves get in the way of absorbing sunlight, nutrients from fertilizers, and water. Feel free to carefully remove some of the foliage to encourage better absorption of nutrients for your broccoli. A good way to know if the foliage is damaging the broccoli rather than helping is to look at the broccoli itself. If the broccoli is growing healthy and strong then the foliage can stay: However, if the inverse is true then you might want to remove some foliage. Do it slowly by getting rid of only a couple leaves at a time so as to not remove too much too fast.

Tips For Pest and Disease Control

Broccoli is the same family as kale and therefore attracts many of the same sort of insects. It is the sweet and dark leafy majority of this robust vegetable that attracts so many insects and small animals to it.

Feel free to spray a forceful stream of water on the broccoli to help drown and wash away insects. You can also cage your broccoli to help deter small animals and birds from eating it. However, the only way to truly protect your broccoli is to provide and spray some sort of insecticide on it. You need to be careful if this is your choice. There is no protective layering on broccoli that will absorb the chemicals from the insecticide. Opt for natural versions or make your own to make sure you are not accidentally poisoning the broccoli, the soil, or yourself.

Harvesting

The broccoli forest will give you the most accurate sign of ripeness. They will be a deep green and colored evenly. If you see yellow in the florist you should harvest the broccoli right away. This will make the broccoli more bitter to taste.

To harvest your broccoli you should do so in the morning. Cut the broccoli at its stem. You can cut it as close to the bunches as you like but make sure that you leave 2 to 3 inches still on the plant. This is to help and encourage re-growth. You should use scissors or a knife; make sure it is as sharp as possible. Dull edges will damage the plant.

Chapter 18

Cabbage

Introduction

Cabbage is often seen as an unpopular vegetable as many individuals only use it in 4 recipes like cabbage rolls. However, cabbage grown in a home garden tastes remarkably different from cabbage grown commercially and bought at the supermarket. It is much easier to chew and digest and it has a sweeter taste to it.

Although growing cabbage in the State of Florida can be a little tricky, if done properly you can improve your relationship with this vegetable to the point where you might like it.

Planting

Planting Instructions From Seeds or Scraps

Growing cabbage from scraps is quite easy to do. Take a healthy head of cabbage, this can be pulled from your garden or from your local supermarket. remove the thick and fibrous outer leaves and place them in the compost. Then cut the head of the cabbage about 3 in above the base. You can use the tops of the cabbage, but the bottom stomp has to regrow.

You can dip the base of the cabbage in a rooting hormone then place it in a small jar or glass of water. You don't want the cabbage cuttings to be completely submerged. Instead you want the water to just cover the base and touch the bottom rounded part of the cabbage stump.

Leave the cabbage in the sun for a few days to a few weeks. Rather quickly you will notice that you are getting regrowth from this cutting. Once you see significant growth, and the roots have grown to about an inch in length, you can plant this cutting into rich soil.

Whether you plant the cabbage in a pot or in the ground it doesn't matter. What matters is the depth. You want the roots to be fully planted into the soil while the area you cut and all pieces of new growth to be just above the soil surface.

Water bottle liberally and allow your cabbage to enjoy a full 8 hours of sun daily.

Planting Instructions From A Shrub

You can also plant cabbage from an already established plant that you've purchased from a greenhouse. Leave the plant outside in your yard for 24-48 hours. Water it well. This will help acclimate the plant to your yard's climate.

Once the cabbage plant has gotten used to your yard's climate, dig a hole that is twice as wide and twice as deep as the pot your shrub came in. Moisten the soil at the bottom of the hole, place your shrub in it, and cover it with enriched soil.

Planting Companions and Planting Mismatches

Companions: Beets, Most Onions, Sage, Celery, Potatoes, Chamomile

Mismatches: Strawberries, Eggplants, Tomatoes

Growing and Care

Cabbage requires a full day and well-watered soil. As you can feel with your hand, cabbage is made up of very durable leaves. This means that cabbage can withstand some of the hotter days that Florida can provide. It enjoys damp soil that doesn't dry out too quickly and that isn't soaked through. What's tricky about watering cabbage is that you want to leave the cabbage itself, the head and the outer leaves, as dry as possible.

This means that when you water it yourself be sure to water the soil surrounding the cabbage and not over the cabbage. When it gets watered by rainfall, be sure to go and look at the cabbage the following day to make sure that the leads are drying out appropriately.

Other than watching for sun and water requirements, cabbage is relatively low maintenance. It will grow enlarged bunches and is pretty resilient to the environment.

Tips For Pest and Disease Control

Cabbage varieties attract a range of different insects. These insects eat away at the leafy parts of the cabbage, leaving giant holes in the vegetable. They can also find their way under the soil surface and eat away at the roots compromising the cabbages growth in general.

Although cabbage doesn't attract any new kind of insect that other vegetables don't attract, cabbages are more susceptible because of how difficult it is to see when infestations occur. The large outer leaves of the Cabbage are folded on top of each other and are open to the sky. This layered structure provides a safe haven for smaller insects. Likewise the rounded and tight center of the cabbage is a favorite place for insects to bury their eggs.

Examine your cabbage regularly and carefully to ensure that no infestation has occurred. If you do find insects you can always forcefully spray water onto the vegetables to drown and wash them away.

Harvesting

The first sign that your cabbage is ready to harvest is that it is firm when you grab it. If the head of the cabbage feels soft or mushy it is too young. You want the leaves to still be tight together with only the outer leaves opening. To harvest your cabbage, using sharp shears, cut the cabbage at the base of the head to remove it from the roots. This stops any regrowth as you take the whole head and the outer leaves. Cut it above the soil. If you want the cabbage to regrow then just cut the head out of the outer leaves.

Chapter 19

Carrots

Introduction

Carrots are perhaps the most basic vegetable anyone can grow in their Garden. However, many individuals grow them incorrectly and end up with thin melee carrots instead of strong thick ones.

Growing carrots in the state of Florida can be challenging due to the temperamental weather and soil, however if you follow the proper instructions you will yield a bountiful and hardy harvest of carrots.

Planting

Planting Instructions From Seeds or Scraps

It is possible to regrow carrots by cutting the stumps. However, most individuals find greater success just simply planting the seeds of carrots. This allows a carrot to be grown from scratch without having to deal with any harm that the previous carrot had.

Carrot seeds are incredibly tiny and therefore only need to be placed shallowly in the soil. In a deep pot sprinkle carrot seeds in a line then carefully cover them with a little bit of nutrient-rich soil. Keep the top layer of soil as moist as possible without completely soaking it. Once you begin to see the growth of your carrots, you can allow the soil to dry out only slightly before watering it again.

Planting Instructions From A Shrub

Planting carrots from previously established plants can be a little tricky. Going against what we've been saying quite often through this book we suggest that you grow your carrots from seeds. What you should also consider is planting your parents where you are going to let them grow. Whether this means keeping them inside or moving the pot outside after you see the germination, the less handling you have of the carrots during their life cycle the more likely you will be successful in growing them.

Planting Companions and Planting Mismatches

Companions: lettuce, most beans and peas, most onions, tomatoes

Mismatches: dill, parsnips

Growing and Care

Since carrots grow under the ground, they are more resilient than other kinds of vegetables because they are protected by the soil. That being said, extreme weather such as sudden cold fronts, droughts or scorching heat, or over-watering due to heavy rainfall can harm your carrots.

The best care advice you can get for growing carrots is to give them as much warm sunlight as possible and keep the soil moist but not what. If you begin to see green sprouting from the soil then your carrots are growing and you need only to continue with your sunlight and watering schedule until you are ready to harvest.

Tips For Pest and Disease Control

Keep in mind that your carrots are growing under the soil which means that the pest that infects them the most are those that live under the soil as well. Unfortunately because you cannot see under the soil it is hard to know if such infestations occur.

The only clues you have are the greens visible to your eye above the soil surface. If they look bright green, are shooting straight up, look strong, are hydrated, and are not willing or discolored then your carrots are most likely safe. However, if your greens are looking ill then your carrots are likely to be attacked.

You can spray pesticides in your garden, but be careful to choose one that is safe for humans. You can also release ladybugs into the garden to eat the smaller insects that can damage your plants.

Harvesting

Unfortunately you won't really know if your carrots are ripe until you pull them from the ground. They are not like apples or tomatoes that you squeeze to test ripeness. But you will likely be able to tell how ripe they are by looking at their ends. If their ends are healthy, thick, and pushed straight out of the ground then they are likely able to be pulled. Most of the time a small head at the top of the carrots will protrude from the soil. This is another sign that they are ready to be picked.

To harvest you can grasp the carrot where the greens meet the carrot and pull straight up. You can also dig around the carrot, using your hands, and loosen the carrots from the soil.

Chapter 20

Cucumbers and Tomatoes

Introduction

Don't let the title of this chapter fool you, cucumbers and tomatoes are not related. However, they are incredibly similar in their growing conditions, how they are harvested, and how they grow in general. For this reason we have combined them in the same chapter.

Planting

Planting Instructions From Seeds or Scraps

It is technically possible to grow cucumbers and tomatoes from their scraps and from seeds. However, it is incredibly difficult to do so, especially in the climate of Florida. The seeds of the cucumber and tomato are incredibly delicate and require careful handling. We highly suggest that you opt against starting your plants with seeds and instead purchase already established cucumber and tomato plants. This way you know that plants can thrive in the Florida climate.

Planting Instructions From A Shrub

Once you've chosen your variety of cucumber or tomato, leave the plant outside in your yard for 24-48 hours. Water it well. This will help acclimate the plant to your yard's climate.

After this 2 day waiting period, you can transplant your tomato and cucumber plants into either a deep pot, into a raised garden bed, or into the ground itself. Tomatoes and cucumbers grow on vines and grow words, or in whatever direction they have support for. Even though your plant will be small, place a small steak or cage around the plant to encourage it to grow. This cage will also provide support for the vine when the heavy tomatoes and cucumbers begin to grow.

Planting Companions and Planting Mismatches

Companions: peas, lettuce, celery

Mismatches: cauliflower, basil, potatoes

Growing and Care

Tomatoes and cucumbers love the sunshine but have leaves that are susceptible to burning and discoloration during the scorching midday sun. You might want to invest in a sort of pergola or system to filter the sunlight onto your tomatoes and cucumbers.

You will also want to keep the soil moist and damp but not soaking. Over-watering is one of the largest downfalls of tomato and cucumber plants.

You will also want to prune both plants. Even though they are not trees, tomatoes and cucumbers have leaves and different vine tendrils that grow in a number of different directions. This means that they can have tendrils and leaves that interfere with the growth of other vegetables.

If you see any leaves or tendrils that are discolored, remove them immediately. Otherwise, if you see any that are growing between two cucumbers or two tomatoes, remove those as well.

Continue with a steady watering and pruning schedule to encourage study and healthy growth.

Tips For Pest and Disease Control

Cucumbers and tomatoes tend to draw in different kinds of beetles and worms that are specific for that kind of vegetable. For example cucumbers don't just attract beetles, they attract cucumber beetles, and tomatoes don't just attract hornworms they attract tomato hornworms.

Thankfully many of these pests are large and can be seen easily. They need to be plucked and removed from the plant as soon as possible. You can also spray your tomato and cucumber plants to drown and wash away smaller insects.

Insecticides are also an option. However, since you will be eating the outside and the inside of the vegetables you want to be careful with which insecticide you choose. There are some that are geared strictly towards tomatoes and cucumbers. These are the commercial varieties you should be looking for. Or you can make your own that are much safer.

Harvesting

Cucumbers

Cucumbers are ripe even when they are of diameter for their entire length, only to taper off at either end. They will have an even green color from end to end and have a firmness to them when squeezed.

Using sharp garden shears or a knife you can cut the cucumber from the vines. Leave some of the small stems on the vine. This will help to encourage regrowth of the cucumbers later on. Some people will say you can twist the cucumbers for free. While this is possible, it is not good for the plant. A straight cut is much better.

Tomatoes

Tomatoes are ripe when they are firm but have a slight give to them. Depending on the varieties they can be red, yellow, orange, green, or even brown. The key here is that they are fully their chosen color without any spots on them.

To harvest a ripe tomato you should be able to simply pluck it directly from the plant. You can also cut them from the plant. Depending on the variety, use one method over the other. For instance, hot house tomatoes are usually picked one at a time. But cherry or grape tomatoes are usually cut off in their bunches.

Chapter 21

Eggplant and Squash

Introduction

Similar to cucumbers and tomatoes, squash has no familial relation in the vegetable world. However, they are very closely linked and are sometimes referred to as one another. This similarity and equivocation of names comes from how similar these plants are in their flavor profiles, cooking methods, and growing conditions.

For this reason we have chosen to bring together eggplant and squash in the same chapter because they have the same growing instructions.

Planting

Planting Instructions From Seeds or Scraps

It is possible to grow eggplants and squash from seedlings, and from cuttings and scraps. In fact many individuals find success in this growing method. However, due to the drastic changes in the Florida climate, we highly suggest you avoid regrowing squash and eggplant yourself. Instead opted to buy a previously established vine from a local greenhouse garden center.

In doing so you will ensure the success of your plants as you can see the eggplant or squash is able to thrive in the environment. In more regulated conditions, growing a plant and squash from scraps is incredibly feasible. However, it becomes difficult when you are trying to choose and decide which variety of these vegetables to grow. It's better to avoid all of this confusion all together and simply plant an established vine shrub.

Planting Instructions From A Shrub

Once you choose your eggplant and squash variety, leave the plant outside in your yard for 24-48 hours. Water it well. This will help acclimate the plant to your yard's climate.

After this you can transplant the vine directly into the ground. Be sure to dig a hole that is twice as deep in twice as large as the pot you received the vegetable in. This will allow for more room for the roots to grow and establish themselves. Keep the soil moist and keep the sun on the plant until you see significant growth. At that point you can back off and water your plant on a schedule.

Planting Companions and Planting Mismatches

Eggplant

Companions: spinach, peppers, potatoes, most beans

Mismatches: fennel

Squash

Companions: most beans, okra, radishes, melons

Mismatches: potatoes

Growing and Care

Squash and eggplant do need quite a bit of water as they enjoy quite a bit of sun. Make sure when you water them that you are watering them deeply, meaning that you are watering the surface as well as the lower levels of soil. This will allow the water to reach its roots.

Eggplants and squash grow in whatever direction they have the most support. Therefore, if you have quite a bit of ground space you can let them spread out and grow directly on the ground. If you do this however you have to be careful not to let the vegetable sit on the ground too long. This can cause it to rot. Alternatively, you can create climbing ladders out of lattice or wood for the plants to grow on. This will allow for the vegetable to be raised above the ground and lessen the chance of it rotting.

The vines and stems grow quite a bit of fibrous leaves. These leaves are meant to protect the vegetable however they can get in the way. If you notice that some of the leaves are hindering the growth of the vegetables, feel free to carefully remove them. However, do so slowly and only remove a couple at a time. Do not want to remove more than you need to as you won't be able to put it back.

Tips For Pest and Disease Control

Although eggplants and squash are susceptible to a variety of insects, the two largest culprits of damage to these vegetables are slugs, snails, and small animals. Slugs and snails feast on the sweet outside of these vegetables and can stay on the vegetables for quite some time.

To help avoid and deter snails, try to keep your squash and eggplant above the ground. Plants that are lying on the ground are more likely to be rotten and therefore attract slugs and snails.

The same actions can help protect your eggplant and squash from smaller animals. As your vegetables lie on the ground and begin to rot they release sweet smelling fumes that attract smaller animals like rodents. By keeping your vegetables growing upwards and supportive you are lessening the chance of your plants becoming rotten and therefore attracting animals.

Harvesting

Eggplant

Your eggplant will be ready to be picked when the color becomes a deep purple. You will also notice that it becomes more firm than squishy. The stem of the eggplant will be a dark brown or gray and will become hard.

Interestingly, this state is before the eggplant is 'ripe'. An eggplant is ripe when the color turns brown. At this point the vegetable is bitter and inedible. Therefore, you have to pick the eggplant before it is ripe.

Using sharp shears or a knife, cut the eggplant from the vine in one slice. There should be a small stem on the released plant, and some stem left on the vine.

Squash

Squash comes in a variety of different colors. Therefore, it can be difficult to tell if your squash is ready by its color. Instead look for the color to become deep and rich. it will also become hard and firm.

To harvest, you need to cut the squash off of the vine. Make sure your utensils are very sharp to avoid harming the stem. Leave 2-3 inches on the squash and some stem on the vine. This will help both the vegetable and the vine stay fresh and avoid rotting.

Chapter 22

Kale

Introduction

Kale gets a bad reputation for being an incredibly tough, chewy, and bitter green. However, many individuals who hold that opinion of kale have only tried kale bought from a supermarket that has been commercially grown. Homegrown kale tastes completely different and it's much sweeter than its commercial counterparts.

When you grow kale from home, you will be able to pick it at its peak flavor to avoid it becoming too bitter. Ultimately, kale is a rather resilient green that, when planted and cared for properly, will return and regrow year after year. In the end it's time for you to give him a second chance by growing it yourself.

Planting

Planting Instructions From Seeds or Scraps

Although it is possible to grow kale from cutting it is incredibly tedious to do so and doesn't work every time. For this reason I highly suggest that you choose an already established plant that has been grown from a seed. This will allow you to bypass any of the potential issues that come with growing kale from a seedling and allow you to enjoy kale much quicker.

Planting Instructions From A Shrub

Leave the plant outside in your yard for 24-48 hours. Water it well. This will help acclimate the plant to your yard's climate.

You can keep the kale in the pot that you got when you bought it or you can plant it into the ground. Either way, make sure that your kale is given quite a bit of sunlight and the soil stays moist.

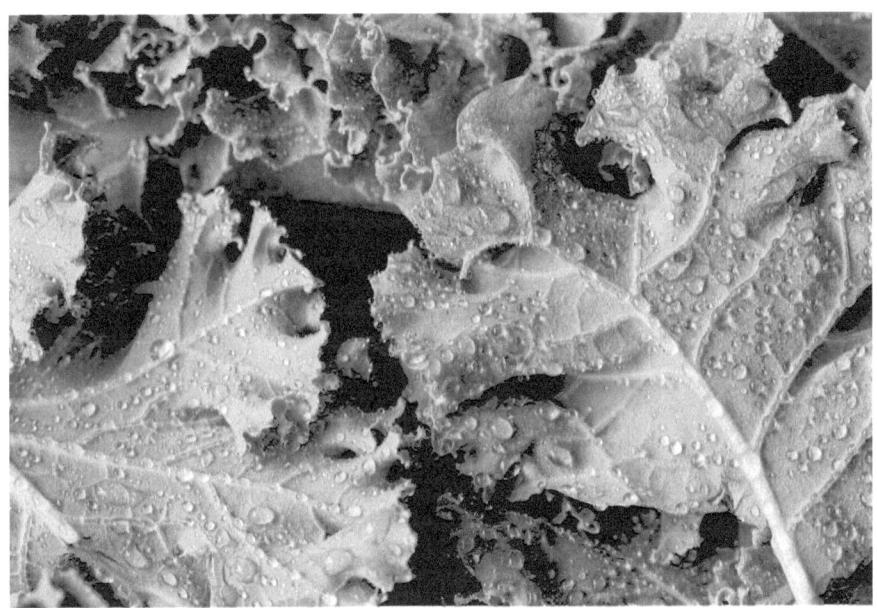

Planting Companions and Planting Mismatches

Companions: Beets, Cucumber, Lettuce, Peas

Mismatches: Other plants at the same time like broccoli and swiss chard

Growing and Care

Growing kale is quite simple. Make sure it gets quite a bit of sun and the water stays moist. That being said, kale can be susceptible to two roads as it will burn some smaller less mature leaves. On the other hand, it is susceptible to overwatering and rot if the leaves can't dry out entirely.

Think about shielding your kale during days where the temperature is incredibly hot. You will also want to follow up with your tale after heavy rain storms to make sure that the leaves are trying properly and are not holding any water.

Other than this careful balancing act, your kale will likely grow stronger in your garden.

Tips For Pest and Disease Control

Like other dark green and leafy vegetables, kale is susceptible to different sorts of worms and beetles. Thankfully, you will be able to inspect the leaves quite easily and notice any sort of infestation because the leaves are so large. As soon as you notice an insect infestation you need to get rid of it. Many of these insects reproduce quite quickly and their population can get out of hand, leading to incredible damage not only to your kale but to your garden in general.

You can spray your greens with a strong and steady stream of water to help drown and wash away the insects - make sure your leaves dry appropriately afterwards.

If you choose to spray insecticide, make sure that they are safe for human ingestion. Here are some at home recipes that use other vegetables as insecticides: these might be your best options.

Harvesting

As kale grows it generally looks the same throughout its life. The color starts off as deep green or purple - depending on the variety - and it has curled edges from the beginning. Therefore, you can tell that kale is ripe by its size. A leaf that is ready to be picked will be about the side of your outstretched hand.

To harvest you need to pull the entire leaf off of the plant: woody stem and all. Kale is rather hardy so you can pull the leaves off or you can cut them. Whatever provides a clean break from the main stem is best. One thing to remember when harvesting kale is to grab the larger outer leaves and not take more than a third of the total plant at one time. If you do, you can hinder the growth of new leaves. You should also never pluck the center leaves as these are the ones that tell the plant to continue to produce leaves.

Chapter 23

Lettuce and Spinach

Introduction

The number of varieties of lettuce and spinach is incredible. Names like romaine, iceberg, and baby spinach are perhaps the most common. But truly there are varieties that come in different flavor profiles, colors, shapes and sizes. Thankfully they all grow under similar conditions and you only need to choose which variety you like best.

Planting

Planting Instructions From Seeds or Scraps

Lettuce and spinach can be grown from scraps. To do so, you first need a full head of lettuce or spinach. Then cut the lettuce about 3 inches above the base. This base will act as a sort of route for regrowth. Place the base of this cutting into a small amount of water and put it in a warm place like a window sill. In about a week's time, you get regrowth. In about two weeks time the lettuce will be ready to harvest once more.

It is important to note that while regrowth from lettuce is rather simple, you will never get the same sort of harvest you did the first time. In fact you can only regrow from a head of lettuce 1 time. For this reason, if you want a full head of lettuce, we highly suggest you start growing lettuce from a previously established lettuce plant that has been grown from seeds.

To get your lettuce plant grown from seeds, go to a greenhouse. It is much easier and will help you avoid any headaches and potential problems in the growing process. Lettuce can be a little fickle in its growth. Choose one that has already sprouted.

Planting Instructions From A Shrub

Once you choose your lettuce variety that has been grown from seeds, leave the plant outside in your yard for 24-48 hours. Water it well. This will help acclimate the plant to your yard's climate.

After this 2 day waiting period, plant your lettuce either in a pot that is slightly larger than the one you purchased it in, or in a hole that is about twice the size of the original pot. This will allow the roots and the lettuce to grow naturally. Put the lettuce in an area that gets direct sun for a full 8 hours a day and make sure that the soil stays damp.

Planting Companions and Planting Mismatches

Companions: carrots, beets, strawberries, radishes

Mismatches: beans, parsley

Growing and Care

Most kinds of lettuce are incredibly delicate. While they enjoy the sun, they shrivel up and burn in scorching heat. On the other hand, they are incredibly susceptible to over-watering and will rot and wilt rather quickly.

Think about protecting your lettuce during the incredibly hot hours of the day and allowing the cooler morning, late afternoon or evening sun to provide nutrients to your lettuce. When it comes to watering you need to be careful with how much you use. If the soil looks dry, be sure to water it just until it becomes moist and dampened. You do not want pools of water collected on the surface of the soil. Lettuce leaves can fall or wilt into the water damaging themselves and in turn damaging the whole head of lettuce.

You will also want to water the base of the lettuce as much as possible and avoid getting the leaves wet. After rainfall check on your status to make sure that the leaves are drying enough. If they are not they can begin to rot. Or, perhaps worse, a droplet of water left on a lettuce leaf can magnify the effects of the hot sun and burn the lettuce.

Tips For Pest and Disease Control

Lettuce and spinach are breeding grounds for insects and pests like worms, beetles, slugs, and snails. Thankfully slugs and snails can be removed by simply picking them off. Moreover, they can be deterred by the use of a gentle insecticide. However, worms and beetles are a little bit more difficult to remove.

You will need to remove them by washing them away and drowning them with a strong stream of water. If you do choose to spray insecticide on your lettuce, make sure it is one that is safe for humans. You don't want to be spraying chemicals all over your lettuce, especially if you're going to be eating it. That's a little counterintuitive for growing your own food.

Harvesting

Lettuce and spinach are usually ripe for picking about two months after planting. You will see brightly colored leaves that have no discoloration. They will stick straight up and look healthy. The outer leaves will be just under 6 inches long.

To harvest lettuce you can either pick individual leaves at a time. Or you can cut the entire head of lettuce at one time. If you do this, make sure you cut it 3 inches above the soil surface level. This will allow you to harvest it at least one more time.

Chapter 24

Mustard and Collard Greens

Introduction

Mustard and collard greens are dark leafy greens that are very present in cooking in the southern United States and the Mediterranean. They are closely related to other vegetables like brussel sprouts in radishes. They have a peppery taste and are usually sauteed to be cooked. They are very resilient greens that pack much more vitamins and taste than the average lettuce.

Once these plants have been established in the garden they will grow bountifully until harvest. If you are a fan of greens such as arugula or swiss chard then you will most likely enjoy mustard and collard greens as well.

Planting

Planting Instructions From Seeds or Scraps

You can regrow mustard and collard greens by propagating a healthy leaf of an established mustard or collard green plant. Cut the bottom of the stem at a 45 degree angle. Dip the end to growth or rooting hormones to encourage new roots. Place the green in a small glass of water: make sure that the water is covering at least two inches of the stem, but have no leaves touching the water. Place the glass in a sunny spot. The window sill is fine.

Replace water when it becomes discolored. You may also want to change your glass to a taller one as your herb grows.

Once you see new roots forming, it is ready to plant.

Plant in a pot, or the ground, with at least two inches under the soil and two inches above the soil. Water daily to make sure the plant stays moist, but don't let water sit. Once you see growth on a consistent basis you can water as needed.

Planting Instructions From A Shrub

If you want to avoid all of this extra work you can always purchase a young mustard or collard green shrub from your local green house.

First, leave the plant outside in your yard for 24-48 hours. Water it well. This will help acclimate the plant to your yard's climate. Then you can plant the vegetable directly into the ground in a hole that is larger than the pot you bought it in: or you can transplant it into a pot that is slightly larger.

Essentially you simply want to give the roots of your mustard or collard greens more room to become established and for the leaves to grow. Keep the soil damp and the leaves in direct sunlight.

Planting Companions and Planting Mismatches

Companions: most beans. broccoli, cabbage, turnips, grapes, cauliflower

Mismatches: doesn't have any known mismatches

Growing and Care

Mustard and collard greens are incredibly sick and robust vegetables. As such they can withstand quite a bit of sun and heat. That being said, if you start to notice shriveled leaves or ones that are turning yellow or brown on the edges, bring shade to your greens. These symptoms mean that it is getting too much sun and is burning.

Since they love quite a bit of sun, they also love quite a bit of water. However, be careful how you water your mustard or collard greens. Water the base of the plant as much as possible and avoid getting water on the actual leaves. Water on the leaves can be absorbed and turn the plant into a pile of rotten greens. If you experience heavy rainfall, double-check on your dark leafy greens to make sure the water is drying up properly. Usually water beads and rolls right off, but there are some cases where it stays and damages the plant.

Tips For Pest and Disease Control

Due to their fibrous nature these dark leafy greens are susceptible to different sorts of worms and beetles. Thankfully, the leaves are quite large and allow for easy inspection. The moment you recognize aphids or any collection of insects and worms you need to act quickly. They multiply at an alarming rate and can eat up an entire head of greens rather quickly.

You can spray your greens with a strong and steady stream of water to help drown and wash away the insects - just be sure your leaves dry appropriately afterwards. You can also spray different insecticides around and on your plants to help deter insects from returning. If you choose to spray insecticide, make sure that they are safe for human ingestion. Indeed you will be washing your leaves before you eat them however you can never be too careful with what you are putting in your body.

Harvesting

Mustard Greens

These greens are usually ripe about a month after planting. The leaves will be larger than your hand and feel almost like velvet. To harvest you only need to cut the larger outer leaves at their stem about an inch above the soil level. You can also cut the entire plant by cutting the leaves about three inches above soil surface level. In doing so you increase your chances of having at least one other harvest.

Collard Greens

The signs for collard greens are very similar to those of mustard greens. However, since you can use the stems of collard greens they usually take longer to mature. They take about 85 days to be ready to be picked. Once they reach the threshold, you can harvest them the same way you harvest mustard greens.

Chapter 25

Turnips

Introduction

Turnips are, interestingly, a part of the mustard family. They have a sweet but peppery taste to them and can be used in a variety of savory and sweet dishes. They're usually considered a cross between a potato and a carrot and are therefore treated as such. They present themselves as a bulb that can be two-toned purple and white or white all over.

They are very closely related to other vegetables like radishes and arugula and follow in the same flavor notes.

Planting

Planting Instructions From Seeds or Scraps

In fact, you can be quite successful in growing turnips from scraps. After you have cut off the tops of healthy turnips, place them with their cut side down in water. Leave them in a sunny and warm area for 3 to 4 days. After this you will begin to notice that small greens are coming from the top and roots are growing from the bottom.

Once you begin to see growth, wait about another week. This will help the routes to establish themselves and gain strength. At this point you can transplant them into the ground or a raised garden bed. You can transplant them into a pot however because they grow under the soil you will need an incredibly deep pot. This is why growing them in a raised garden bed or directly into the ground is preferred.

Planting Instructions From A Shrub

If you do not want to wait two weeks to grow your turnips from your cuttings, you can always purchase young turnip plants from a local greenhouse.

Leave the plant outside in your yard for 24-48 hours. Water it well. This will help acclimate the plant to your yard's climate. Usually the container you buy turnips in is large enough to allow them to grow there for their entire lifespan. However, if you do transplant your turn up please do so incredibly carefully. There will not be a lot of substance to plant and you do not want to damage any of the young roots.

When you transplant, make sure that the entire head and roots of the turnip are just below the soil surface, with the greens coming up and protruding out words. If you see a little bit at the top of the turnip that is okay. You don't want to plant them incredibly deep. Keep the soil moist and the plant in direct sunlight.

Planting Companions and Planting Mismatches

Companions: mint, peas

Mismatches: Not known to dislike any crop

Growing and Care

Sims turnips grow underneath the soil you want to make sure the soil under the surface is taken care of. They need about 1 inch of water a week. If you notice the top of the soil getting a little dry, there is no need to panic. If you press on the soil and it is still moist underneath you can wait another day for rainfall or a watery. It is the lower levels of soil that are important.

Another consequence of turnips growing under the soil is that they can handle quite a bit of sunlight. However, if the leaves of the turnip plant become brittle, provide some sort of shade or sun relief for your turnip.

Tips For Pest and Disease Control

Turnips are incredibly susceptible to aphids and maggots. This is largely due to the fact that they grow in the most soil. They are also susceptible to different kinds of plague and mold for the same reason. Make sure that your soil is draining well and it is not holding on to any unnecessary water. Likewise, make sure there's no water sitting on the surface of the soil. This is a breeding ground for pests and diseases. You can notice damage by looking at the greens. If there is anything wrong with the greens of the turnip there's likely something wrong with the turn of itself. You might need to spray the soil with insecticides or and traduce a family of ladybugs or insect eating bugs to munch on the pests.

Harvesting

It can be difficult to tell when turnips are ready to be picked because they grow under the ground. All you have to go on is the ripeness signs of their leaves. Usually turnips are ready to be picked up about a month-and-a-half after planting. If you are just harvesting the leaves you can harvest them well before that however. Similar to carrots, the leaves of the turnips should be strong and pointing upward. There should be no discoloration and no wilting leaves. You will also be able to see the tops of the turnips as they push up just above soil surface level.

To harvest the turnips you need only to gently pull them out of the soil by grasping the leaves closest to the top of the turnip. It is highly suggested that you harvest turnips when the soil is dry this will allow for easier harvesting and cleaning.

Part Four

Nuts, Herbs, and Miscellaneous

Chapter 26

Basil

Introduction

Basil is one of the more versatile herbs worldwide, and has a number of different varieties. Some of these varieties include sweet basil, purple basil, and Thai basil. Although they have different flavors and tasting notes, they can all follow the same growing instructions.

Planting

Planting Instructions From Seeds or Scraps

Choose a long healthy stem from an established basil plant. Gently pull it from the soil or cut it away from the mother plant. Remove all the leaves and leave only about two inches worth of leaves at the top.

Cut the bottom of the stem at a 45 degree angle. Dip the end to growth or rooting hormones to encourage new roots. Place the herb in a small glass of water: make sure that the water is covering at least two inches of the stem, but have no leaves touching the water. Place the glass in a sunny and warm spot - a window sill that gets full sun will do just fine for this.

Replace water as needed: you may also want to change your glass to a taller one as your herb grows.

Once you see new roots forming, and you begin to see new leaves, your basil is ready to plant.

Plant in a pot, or the ground, with at least two inches under the soil and two inches above the soil. Water daily to make sure the plant stays moist, but don't let water sit.

Once you see growth on a consistent basis you can water as needed.

Planting Instructions From A Shrub

Leave the plant outside in your yard for 24-48 hours. Water it well. This will help acclimate the plant to your yard's climate.

You can keep the herb in the pot or plant in the ground: just make sure at least inches are under the soil and at least two inches are above the ground. Make sure your basil is in a sunny area that gets some shade in the evening and morning. Too much sun can burn the delicate leaves.

Water basil daily but be careful not to over water. Once you see consistent growth you can water as needed.

Planting Companions and Planting Mismatches

Companions: Sweet peppers, tomatoes, asparagus and oregano.

Mismatches: Sage

Growing and Care

Basil is one of the more delicate herbs out there. This means that although it loves full sun, it is rather susceptible to burning in scorching sun and wilting due to over watering.

To care for your basil, keep it in a warm area with direct sunlight. However, keep it in the shade during midday. You also need to be careful about overwatering. If you are keeping the plant inside, let the top of the soil become a little dry before watering. If you press on the soil it should be damp; water only a little bit at a time so as to not soak the roots.

Also, if you can, water it from the base and don't let water sit on the leaves.

Tips For Pest and Disease Control

When it comes to basil, the two most common pests are slugs and Japanese beetles. These two bugs make basil a skeleton of its former self as they will eat the leaves but will leave any vein or stem of the plant.

Thankfully these pests are relatively easy to get rid of. Slugs can be removed by simply picking them up and moving them. They can also be deterred by sprinkling a little bit of coffee grounds, sand, or even ashes from burned wood around the bottom of your plant.

The smaller bugs that are drawn to basil don't have a strong connection to the plant, this means that simply spraying your basil plant with a mist of water will help to remove any other bug.

You can also spray with insecticides, but be careful about how dangerous those substances are to humans.

Harvesting

To harvest, you can either pick individual leaves from your plant or you can pull out filler sprigs from the plant. Try to take it from the top first to continue to encourage regrowth.

Know that if you take from the roots, that root will not regrow. Instead, if you need to take more at a time, think about cutting your plant about three to four inches above soil level.

If you find that the plant is drying out, you can always take the whole plant, dry out the leaves, and blend it to create a dry spice.

Chapter 27

Chestnuts, Pecans, and Walnut Trees

Introduction

Nuts like chestnuts, pecans, and walnuts are incredibly healthy foods. Thankfully even though they are all different kinds of nuts they all grow on trees and relatively under the same conditions. This means that you will simply have to choose which variety of not you want to grow and then follow the same instructions. That being said, there are certain varieties of these nuts that should be avoided. For example, horse chestnuts should be avoided. Black walnuts should be avoided if you have animals on the property. Black walnuts, while being safe to eat for humans, can be toxic to canines, felines, and other animals.

Planting

Planting Instructions From Seeds or Scraps

Almost every nut tree, including chestnuts, pecans, and walnuts, can be grown from seeds. However, like many of the other foods in this book, the Florida climate can be unforgiving to seed growth.

Therefore it is suggested that you purchase already sprouted seeds to grow your own nut trees. You are more likely to find success in your own backyard garden if you do this. Of course if you have the support of a commercial farm feel free to grow them from seeds. However, nut trees take a while to produce the product, getting a head start by purchasing an already sprouted plant will help you not only be more successful but to get nuts sooner.

Planting Instructions From A Shrub

Once you choose the nut variety that you would like, leave the plant outside in your yard for 24-48 hours. Water it well. This will help acclimate the plant to your yard's climate.

You can keep the shrub in the pot given to you, however, because it is a tree that will likely want to transplant it into a larger pot or into the ground. For this latter option dig a hole twice as deep and twice as wide as the pot the tree originally came in. Moisten the soil in the hole, plant the tree, and cover with more soil.

Planting Companions and Planting Mismatches

Chestnuts

Companions: Tulips, and any trees of the ash or oak varieties

Mismatches: Tomatoes

Pecans

Companions: Stone fruits like peaches and plums, grapes, raspberries

Mismatches: walnut trees, eucalyptus

Walnuts

Companions: Most onions, most melons, carrots, beets

Mismatches: asparagus, rhubarb, cabbage

Growing and Care

Until your nut tree becomes established, caring for it can be a tricky business. They love the sun but are intolerant of scorching heat. They can also be damaged by high winds, strong rain, or over-watering.

Planting your nut tree around other trees will help the sunlight be filtered and not so damaging to the leaves. Try not to overwater the plant while it is being established as you will flood the roots.

However, once the tree has been established and has a good root system, it is pretty indestructible.

Tips For Pest and Disease Control

Gall wasps are one of the largest annoyances when it comes to growing nut trees. They are attracted to the sweet scent of the flowers. Unfortunately these wasps can stop and delay the sprouting and growth of the actual nut on the tree.

You will see the wasps themselves or you will see small areas of swelling on the leaves and branches of your trees.

You can get rid of these wasps by either spraying the tree with a specific gall wasp spray to kill them, or by cutting off the infected branches and burning them.

That being said, gall wasps are tricky and can be dangerous to remove; they tend to sting and get aggressive when provoked. For this reason many people hire professionals to get rid of them.

Harvesting

Chestnuts

Unlike fruits and vegetables that need to be picked from their respective plants and branches, chestnuts fall to the ground when they are ready to be harvested.

You only need to pick them off of the ground. They will be in small collections with burs and spikes on them. Carefully remove the nuts from these burs and store them however you wish.

Pecans

It can be difficult to know when pecans are ripe to be picked. Like chestnuts they will release themselves from the tree and fall to the ground. However, one way to know if there are potentially ripe nuts that have yet to fall is to gently shake and jostle the tree. This will encourage the right pecans to fall. You only need to collect them and bring them inside. Be careful not to shake the tree too much and be sure to get rid of any nuts that look like they have been damaged or infested by bugs.

Walnuts

Walnuts, like the two nuts mentioned before it, will fall to the ground when right. However, you can encourage ripe walnuts to release their hold by using a pool to shake the branches. Be very careful not to harm any of the budding nuts or blooms.

Chapter 28

Cilantro

Introduction

Cilantro is a rather dividing herb. Individuals either love it or they hate it. Interestingly, those people that don't like it are said to have a gene that makes the herb taste like soap. Fortunately, growing cilantro isn't as complicated as deciding its taste profile.

Planting

Planting Instructions From Seeds or Scraps

Choose a long healthy stem from an established cilantro plant. Gently pull it from the soil or cut it away from the mother plant. Remove all the leaves and leave only about two inches worth of leaves at the top.

Cut the bottom of the stem at a 45 degree angle. Dip the end to growth or rooting hormones to encourage new roots. Place the herb in a small glass of water: make sure that the water is covering at least two inches of the stem, but have no leaves touching the water. Place the glass in a sunny and warm spot - a window sill that gets full sun will do just fine for this.

Replace water as needed: you may also want to change your glass to a taller one as your herb grows.

Once you see new roots forming, and you begin to see new leaves, your cilantro is ready to plant.

Plant in a pot, or the ground, with at least two inches under the soil and two inches above the soil. Water daily to make sure the plant stays moist but does not let water sit.

Once you see growth on a consistent basis you can water as needed.

Planting Instructions From A Shrub

Leave the plant outside in your yard for 24-48 hours. Water it well. This will help acclimate the plant to your yard's climate.

You can keep the herb in the pot or plant in the ground: just make sure at least inches are under the soil and at least two inches are above the ground. Make sure your cilantro is in a sunny area that gets some shade in the evening and morning. Too much sun can burn the delicate leaves.

Water cilantro daily but be careful not to over water. Once you see consistent growth you can water as needed.

Planting Companions and Planting Mismatches

Companions: most other herbs including basil, parsley

Mismatches: any plant that grows fruit, this includes tomatoes, sweet peppers, berries, or cucumbers.

Growing and Care

Like most herbs, cilantro loves the sun. However, you should be careful about your leaves burning. Keep your cilantro in a pot and move it around the yard to ensure the scorching sun doesn't get at it. If you planted the herb on the ground, consider sun protection that is removable or planting your cilantro near a tree to filter the sun.

Keep the soil moist, but not wet. If you start noticing your leaves turning yellow or discolored, you may need to reconsider where you've planted it.

Tips For Pest and Disease Control

The good news for cilantro is that the smell and taste tends to repel most insects and bugs, including spiders and spider mites.

However, cilantro is prone to different diseases and kinds of rot. To avoid this you should try your best to water your plant at the base and not allow water to sit on the leaves. If you have planted the herb outside, and cannot avoid rainfall falling on the leaves, then watch out for water droplets that do not run off or sit on the leaves.

Harvesting

To harvest, you can either pick individual leaves from your plant or you can pull out filler sprigs from the plant. Try to take it from the top first to continue to encourage regrowth.

Know that if you take from the roots, that root will not regrow. Instead, if you need to take more at a time, think about cutting your plant about three to four inches above soil level.

If you find that the plant is drying out, you can always take the whole plant, dry out the leaves, and blend it to create a dry spice.

Chapter 29

Dill

Introduction

Dill is an incredibly versatile herb that is oftentimes forgotten. Unless used regularly, it is usually missing from the pantries of the everyday chef. However, by growing it yourself you will always have some on hand to spice up any meal.

Planting

Planting Instructions From Seeds or Scraps

Choose a long healthy stem from an established dill plant. Gently pull it from the soil or cut it away from the mother plant. Remove all the leaves and leave only about two inches worth of leaves at the top.

Cut the bottom of the stem at a 45 degree angle. Dip the end to growth or rooting hormones to encourage new roots. Place the herb in a small glass of water: make sure that the water is covering at least two inches of the stem, but have no leaves touching the water. Place the glass in a sunny and warm spot - a window sill that gets full sun will do just fine for this.

Replace water as needed: you may also want to change your glass to a taller one as your herb grows.

Once you see new roots forming, and you begin to see new leaves, your dill is ready to plant.

Plant in a pot, or the ground, with at least two inches under the soil and two inches above the soil. Water daily to make sure the plant stays moist but does not let water sit.

Once you see growth on a consistent basis you can water as needed.

Planting Instructions From A Shrub

Leave the plant outside in your yard for 24-48 hours. Water it well. This will help acclimate the plant to your yard's climate.

You can keep the herb in the pot or plant in the ground: just make sure at least inches are under the soil and at least two inches are above the ground. Make sure your dill is in a sunny area that gets some shade in the evening and morning. Too much sun can burn the delicate leaves.

Water it daily, but be careful not to overwater. Once you see consistent growth you can water as needed.

Planting Companions and Planting Mismatches

Companions: Asparagus, Corn, Cucumbers, most onions, Lettuce

Mismatches: most pepper plants, including sweet and spicy varieties, carrots, fennel

Growing and Care

Dill loves the sun. Since it has smaller leaves it is more resilient to harsh sunlight than other herbs. Watering the soil and making sure it stays moist will help your dill be even more hardy in the Florida sunlight.

Try not to let water sit at the base of the plant. Sitting water can breed mold and attract insects and bugs.

Harvesting

To harvest, you can either pick individual leaves from your plant or you can pull out full sprigs from the plant. Try to take it from the top first to continue to encourage regrowth.

Know that if you take from the roots, that root will not regrow. Instead, if you need to take more at a time, think about cutting your plant about three to four inches above soil level.

If you find that the plant is drying out, you can always take the whole plant, dry out the leaves, and blend it to create a dry spice.

Tips For Pest and Disease Control

Aphids are the most common pests for dill plants; whether they are indoors or outdoors. Although they are relatively harmless for your dill plant because there are too many leaves, and can be removed easily, they multiply incredibly fast. This means that they can jump from your dill plants to other plants where they can be more dangerous.

To avoid this you can make sure that you are spraying your water from the top down. This will allow the aphids to be washed away and drowned by the stream.

Chapter 30

Ginger

Introduction

Ginger is an important and healthy root to have in your kitchen. It can help lower blood sugars, deter nausea, and even lower cholesterol. It has a spicy and peppery taste that many find enjoyable. However, the taste can also be hidden or masked for those who are not fond of the taste.

Planting

Planting Instructions From Seeds or Scraps

Soak your ginger in water for 24 hours. This will help to wash the skin and remove preservatives from the store. Leave it on the counter to dry for 24 hours.

Prepare your soil by mixing in either homemade or commercial fertilizers.

Cut the ginger into pieces that are about one inch long. Do not peel the ginger and try to choose pieces that have 'eyes' on them. It is from these eyes that new ginger will grow. Cut the ginger into pieces that are about one inch long. Leave the pieces out for at least 24 hours so the cut side can form a callus. This may take a few days.

Plant the ginger about 2-4 inches under the soil with the cut side up. If you see buds forming make sure that these buds are facing towards the sky. Place your plant in a warm sunny spot; ginger needs lots of sun.

Planting Instructions From A Shrub

Leave the plant outside in your yard for 24-48 hours. Water it well. This will help acclimate the plant to your yard's climate.

From here you can leave it in the pot, transplant it into a larger pot, or plant it into the ground. If you transplant it, be sure to use a bigger pot than it came in as the plant will likely grow. Ginger can grow up to three feet tall.

Planting Companions and Planting Mismatches

Companions: lemon grass, chilies, lilies

Mismatches: does not have any known mismatches

Growing and Care

Even though ginger loves sun it equally loves water. Make sure the soil stays moist and not soaking wet. Sitting water is a death sentence for ginger.

Your ginger grows under the ground and will have its stems and leaves protrude above the soil. If your soil is too wet or too dry then you will have weak and wrinkly ginger.

Tips For Pest and Disease Control

Since your ginger is growing underground it is at the mercy of those bugs that live under the soil. This can also make it harder to notice any bugs eating your ginger until it is too late.

Keep an eye on the leaves and stems that grow out of the ground. Damaged leaves, discoloration, or wilting stems are signs that there are sinister insects down below.

You can spray pesticides in your garden, but be careful to choose one that is safe for humans. However, you can also release ladybugs into the garden. They will eat the smaller insects that can damage your plants (Ginger Pests Problems).

Harvesting

To harvest your ginger you only need to dig up the entire plant. Using your hands as tools can harm the spices, dig into the soil about 6 inches all around the plant. Gently pull out the spice and brush off any soil that is left on it. You can harvest ginger at any point in the growing process but it is ideal for it to be harvested about 10 months after planting.

Although you will be digging up the whole plant, you will be able to use the scraps to grow it again.

Chapter 31

Lemon Balm

Introduction

Lemon balm is very similar to lemon grass but it is much easier to work with. It has a much milder flavor than its lemon herb relatives and acts like any conventional herb, meaning that it follows most of the same growing requirements.

Planting

Planting Instructions From Seeds or Scraps

Choose a long healthy stem from an established lemon balm plant. Gently pull it from the soil or cut it away from the mother plant. Remove all the leaves and leave only about two inches worth of leaves at the top.

Cut the bottom of the stem at a 45 degree angle. Dip the end to encourage new roots. Place the herb in a small glass of water: make sure that the water is covering at least two inches of the stem, but have no leaves touching the water. Place the glass in a sunny and warm spot - a window sill that gets full sun will do just fine for this.

Replace water as needed: you may also want to change your glass to a taller one as your herb grows.

Once you see new roots forming, and you begin to see new leaves, your lemon balm is ready to plant.

Plant in a pot, or the ground, with at least two inches under the soil and two inches above the soil. Water daily to make sure the plant stays moist but do not let water sit.

Once you see growth on a consistent basis you can water as needed.

Planting Instructions From A Shrub

Leave the plant outside in your yard for 24-48 hours. Water it well. This will help acclimate the plant to your yard's climate.

You can keep the herb in the pot or plant in the ground: just make sure at least inches are under the soil and at least two inches are above the ground. Make sure your lemon balm is in a sunny area that gets some shade in the evening and morning. Too much sun can burn the delicate leaves.

Water your lemon balm daily but be careful not to over water. Once you see consistent growth you can water as needed.

Planting Companions and Planting Mismatches

Companions: most kinds of squash, most melon variety, tomatoes, most apples trees, onions

Mismatched: does not grow well when planted in the same soil as other herbs.

Growing and Care

Lemon balm, as being a part of the mint family, is an incredibly hardy and resilient herb. It will grow in most growing conditions no matter the amount of sunlight or water conditions. In fact, once lemon balm has established its root base in the soil, it will likely take over any area you plant it in.

To ensure that your lemon balm is healthy, keep it in a warm sunny place and water frequently. Like most every other food plant, avoid water pooling at the base and limit scorching sunlight.

Tips For Pest and Disease Control

Aphids are the most dangerous pests. They are drawn to the sweet smell and taste of this herb. Since lemon balm has large flat leaves, aphids have a lot to munch on.

Insecticides are your best bet to get rid of these pests. You can also spray your plant with a strong stream of water from a hose to drown and wash them away. If there are only a few you can also take them off manually or simply pull the infected stalk of lemon balm out of the ground entirely.

Harvesting

To harvest, you can either pick individual leaves from your plant or you can pull out filler sprigs from the plant. Try to take it from the top first to continue to encourage regrowth.

Know that if you take from the roots, that root will not regrow. Instead, if you need to take more at a time, think about cutting your plant about three to four inches above soil level.

If you find that the plant is drying out, you can always take the whole plant, dry out the leaves, and blend it to create a dry spice.

Chapter 32

Mint

Introduction

Mint is one of the most popular herbs found in any garden. It is hardy and will grow under most conditions. In fact mint is one herb that will grow and regrow year after year, season after season. As such, it is a very low maintenance herb that even the most inexperienced gardeners can grow successfully.

Planting

Planting Instructions From Seeds or Scraps

Choose a long healthy stem from an established mint plant. Gently pull it from the soil or cut it away from the mother plant. Remove all the leaves and leave only about two inches worth of leaves at the top.

Cut the bottom of the stem at a 45 degree angle. Dip the end to growth or rooting hormones to encourage new roots. Place the herb in a small glass of water: make sure that the water is covering at least two inches of the stem, but have no leaves touching the water. Place the glass in a sunny and warm spot - a window sill that gets full sun will do just fine for this.

Replace water as needed: you may also want to change your glass to a taller one as your herb grows.

Once you see new roots forming, and you begin to see new leaves, your mint is ready to plant.

Plant in a pot, or the ground, with at least two inches under the soil and two inches above the soil. Water daily to make sure the plant stays moist but do not let water sit.

Once you see growth on a consistent basis you can water as needed.

Planting Instructions From A Shrub

Leave the plant outside in your yard for 24-48 hours. Water it well. This will help acclimate the plant to your yard's climate.

You can keep the herb in the pot or plant in the ground: just make sure at least inches are under the soil and at least two inches are above the ground. Make sure your mint is in a sunny area that gets some shade in the evening and morning. Too much sun can burn the delicate leaves.

Water mint daily but be careful not to over water. Once you see consistent growth you can water as needed.

Note: mint takes over wherever you plant it. It does well in a pot or in a well contained area in the ground

Planting Companions and Planting Mismatches

Companions: Oregano, Carrots, kale, Tomatoes, most Peas and beans.

Mismatches: lavender, rosemary, sage, oregano, and thyme

Growing and Care

Mint loves the sun. Make sure you keep your mint in as sunny of a place as possible. However, with such love for the sun it is easy for the soil to dry out. Make sure your soil is well-trained and moist.

Thankfully once mint establishes itself it will be very hard to get rid of. Be sure to prune and pull any overgrowth often to contain your herbs from taking over other plants.

Tips For Pest and Disease Control

Similar to lemon balm, which is a part of the mint family, aphids are the most common insect. You can read your plants of aphids by using the same methods as you do with lemon balm.

However, mint is also prone to caterpillars. You can spray your mint with a soap and water substance to help deter these pests. The caterpillars will ingest the leaves covered with soapy water, die and fall off your plant.

Harvesting

To harvest, you can either pick individual leaves from your plant or you can pull out filler sprigs from the plant. Try to take it from the top first to continue to encourage regrowth.

Know that if you take from the roots, that root will not regrow. Instead, if you need to take more at a time, think about cutting your plant about three to four inches above soil level.

If you find that the plant is drying out, you can always take the whole plant, dry out the leaves, and blend it to create a dry spice.

Chapter 33

Oregano

Introduction

Oregano is an herb used in the Mediterranean in parts of Italy. It has a very mild peppery taste to it. Although for some people oregano does have too strong of a taste. For these individuals, the spice marjoram is highly recommended. Both oregano and marjoram grow under the same conditions.

Planting

Planting Instructions From Seeds or Scraps

Choose a long healthy stem from an established oregano plant. Gently pull it from the soil or cut it away from the mother plant. Remove all the leaves and leave only about two inches worth of leaves at the top.

Cut the bottom of the stem at a 45 degree angle. Dip the end to growth or rooting hormones to encourage new roots. Place the herb in a small glass of water: make sure that the water is covering at least two inches of the stem, but have no leaves touching the water. Place the glass in a sunny and warm spot - a window sill that gets full sun will do just fine for this.

Replace water as needed: you may also want to change your glass to a taller one as your herb grows.

Once you see new roots forming, and you begin to see new leaves, your oregano is ready to plant.

Plant in a pot, or the ground, with at least two inches under the soil and two inches above the soil. Water daily to make sure the plant stays moist but do not let water sit.

Once you see growth on a consistent basis you can water as needed.

Planting Instructions From A Shrub

Leave the plant outside in your yard for 24-48 hours. Water it well. This will help acclimate the plant to your yard's climate.

You can keep the herb in the pot or plant in the ground: just make sure at least inches are under the soil and at least two inches are above the ground. Make sure your oregano is in a sunny area that gets some shade in the evening and morning. Too much sun can burn the delicate leaves.

Water oregano daily but be careful not to over water. Once you see consistent growth you can water as needed.

Planting Companions and Planting Mismatches

Companions: broccoli, brussels sprouts, cabbage, cauliflower, collard greens, kale, turnips

Mismatches: basil, chives, cilantro, mint

Growing and Care

Oregano loves sunlight. Unfortunately the delicate leaves of oregano are susceptible to burning. This means that you should plant oregano in an area that receives shade during the scorching midday hours. You can also plan to oregano under a tree that will help filter the sunlight, or in a pot that you can move around to avoid burning the leaves.

You also need to be careful of over-watering. Although the taste of oregano is incredibly strong, the plant itself is rather delicate. Too much water can lead to wilting oregano or oregano that has a weak flavor.

Tips For Pest and Disease Control

Spider mites are the most common insect for oregano. They enjoy the spicy flavor of the leaves and stem. To make matters worse, spider mites multiply quite quickly so if you do not get an infestation under control then your entire plant can be damaged.

If you do not want to use insecticide the best way to control spider mites, you can spray your oregano plant with a strong stream of water from a hose. Heavy rainfall can also achieve the same result. You can spray your oregano plant with a combination of soapy water or any more oil to help increase the effectiveness of your efforts.

Harvesting

To harvest, you can either pick individual leaves from your plant or you can pull out filler sprigs from the plant. Try to take it from the top first to continue to encourage regrowth.

Know that if you take from the roots, that root will not regrow. Instead, if you need to take more at a time, think about cutting your plant about three to four inches above soil level.

If you find that the plant is drying out, you can always take the whole plant, dry out the leaves, and blend it to create a dry spice.

Chapter 34

Parsley

Introduction

There are a number of varieties of parsley. What makes them different is where they originated from. However, for those who are not well-versed in the geography of parsley, there are two general types. Flat leaf and curly. Varieties that have flat leaves are usually more robust in their flavor whereas curly parsley is usually used as decoration or as a finishing herb.

No matter the variety, almost every parsley kind will grow the same way.

Planting

Planting Instructions From Seeds or Scraps

Choose a long healthy stem from an established parsley plant. Gently pull it from the soil or cut it away from the mother plant. Remove all the leaves and leave only about two inches worth of leaves at the top.

Cut the bottom of the stem at a 45 degree angle. Dip the end in growth or rooting hormone to encourage new roots. Place the herb in a small glass of water: make sure that the water is covering at least two inches of the stem, but have no leaves touching the water. Place the glass in a sunny and warm spot - a window sill that gets full sun will do just fine for this.

Replace water as needed: you may also want to change your glass to a taller one as your herb grows.

Once you see new roots forming, and you begin to see new leaves, your parsley is ready to plant.

Plant in a pot, or the ground, with at least two inches under the soil and two inches above the soil. Water daily to make sure the plant stays moist but do not let water sit.

Once you see growth on a consistent basis you can water as needed.

Planting Instructions From A Shrub

Leave the plant outside in your yard for 24-48 hours. Water it well. This will help acclimate the plant to your yard's climate.

You can keep the herb in the pot or plant in the ground: just make sure at least inches are under the soil and at least two inches are above the ground. Make sure your parsley is in a sunny area that gets some shade in the evening and morning. Too much sun can burn the delicate leaves.

Water parsley daily but be careful not to over water. Once you see consistent growth you can water as needed.

Planting Companions and Planting Mismatches

Companions: Tomatoes, Chives, Carrots, most pepper varieties, most onions varieties, most pea varieties

Mismatches: mint, most lettuce varieties

Growing and Care

Parsley, although versatile, can be delicate. The tiny leaves can burn easily and be damaged by sun, wind, water, and frost.

For eBay results, you should keep your parsley in a pot that you can take home, or move around your yard to help keep it in sunlight, but to protect it. Scorching hot midday sun is not the best for parsley plants.

Be sure not to over water your parsley. The soil should stay damp but not soak. If you are noticing puddles in the soil it means that the soil and the roots are already filled with water and cannot absorb any more. In other words if you see puddles, that is too much water.

Tips For Pest and Disease Control

Parsley is susceptible to most other kinds of tests than other herbs are. However, parsley is most susceptible to what is known as parsley worm. These are large caterpillar looking insects that like to crawl along the stems of the plant and eat the leaves.

Thankfully these caterpillars don't multiply quickly and can be removed by somebody picking them off by him. All you need to do is keep an eye out for them so they don't eat too many leaves before you remove them.

Harvesting

To harvest, you can either pick individual leaves from your plant or you can pull out filler sprigs from the plant. Try to take from the top first to continue to encourage regrowth.

Know that if you take from the roots, that root will not regrow. Instead, if you need to take more at a time, think about cutting your plant about three to four inches above soil level.

If you find that the plant is drying out, you can always take the whole plant, dry out the leaves, and blend it to create a dry spice.

Chapter 35

Rosemary

Introduction

Rosemary is an herb that originated in the Mediterranean and is part of the mint family. This makes it an incredibly hardy herb that is easy and resilient to grow.

Rosemary grows best in a pot but can also have incredibly deep and established routes when grown in the ground. It really depends on your garden landscape and how well you are able to contain your rosemary.

Planting

Planting Instructions From Seeds or Scraps

Choose a long healthy stem from an established rosemary plant. Gently pull it from the soil or cut it away from the mother plant. Remove all the leaves and leave only about two inches worth of leaves at the top.

Cut the bottom of the stem at a 45 degree angle. Dip the end in growth or rooting hormone to encourage new roots. Place the herb in a small glass of water: make sure that the water is covering at least two inches of the stem, but have no leaves touching the water. Place the glass in a

sunny and warm spot - a window sill that gets full sun will do just fine for this.

Replace water as needed: you may also want to change your glass to a taller one as your herb grows.

Once you see new roots forming, and you begin to see new leaves, your rosemary is ready to plant.

Plant in a pot, or the ground, with at least two inches under the soil and two inches above the soil. Water daily to make sure the plant stays moist but do not let water sit.

After you see growth on a consistent basis you can water as needed.

Planting Instructions From A Shrub

Leave the plant outside in your yard for 24-48 hours. Water it well. This will help acclimate the plant to your yard's climate.

You can keep the herb in the pot or plant in the ground: just make sure at least inches are under the soil and at least two inches are above the ground. Make sure your rosemary is in a sunny area that gets some shade in the evening and morning. Too much sun can burn the delicate leaves.

Water rosemary daily but be careful not to over water. Once you see consistent growth you can water as needed.

Planting Companions and Planting Mismatches

Companions: most bean varieties, broccoli, most cabbage varieties, carrots, most hot pepper varieties

Mismatches: cucumbers, watermelon, corn, celery, most pumpkin and squash varieties, tomatoes

Growing and Care

Due to rosemary's sturdy stem and long leaves it can take a lot of sunlight. That being said, the more sunlight a plant likes the more water it needs. Make sure that the soil stays moist but not soaking wet. Although rosemary is hardy and resilient it does not do well with standing water in its soil.

If you grow your rosemary in a pot, feel free to move it around your garden to ensure that it is getting sunlight, however it is not burning.

Tips For Pest and Disease Control

Rosemary is acceptable to most every pest. Beware of root rot. Because rosemary has such a woody stem, it can be more susceptible to different kinds of disease.

This usually creates limp and flimsy rosemary as opposed to the strong and sturdy stems we know it to have. To avoid root rot you can spray your rosemary with a mixture of water and baking soda. This will help to distribute the nutrients in the soil up into the roots of the rosemary

Harvesting

To harvest you can either pick individual leaves from your plant or you can pull out filler sprigs from the plant. Try to take from the top first to continue to encourage regrowth.

Know that if you take from the roots, that root will not regrow. Instead, if you need to take more at a time, think about cutting your plant about three to four inches above soil level.

If you find that the plant is drying out, you can always take the whole plant, dry out the leaves, and blend it to create a dry spice.

Chapter 36

Sage

Introduction

There are many different kinds of sage however this herb is usually characterized by its large and almost fuzzy leaves. Nearly all varieties of sage have a sweet yet earthy flavor to them which allows it to be paired with both savory and sweet food.

No matter the kind of sage you planned they will all follow the same sort of growing instructions.

Planting

Planting Instructions From Seeds or Scraps

Choose a long healthy stem from an established sage plant. Gently pull it from the soil or cut it away from the mother plant. Remove all leaves and leave only about two inches worth of leaves at the top.

Cut the bottom of the stem at a 45 degree angle. Dip the end in growth or rooting hormone to encourage new roots. Place the herb in a small glass of water; make sure that the water is covering at least two inches of the stem, but have no leaves touching the water. Place the glass in a

sunny and warm spot - a window sill that gets full sun will do just fine for this.

Replace water as needed: you may also want to change your glass to a taller one as your herb grows.

Once you see new roots forming, and you begin to see new leaves, your sage is ready to plant.

Plant in a pot, or the ground, with at least two inches under the soil and two inches above the soil. Water daily to make sure the plant stays moist but do not let water sit.

After you see growth on a consistent basis you can water as needed.

Planting Instructions From A Shrub

Leave the plant outside in your yard for 24-48 hours. Water it well. This will help acclimate the plant to your yard's climate.

You can keep the herb in the pot or plant in the ground: just make sure at least inches are under the soil and at least two inches are above the ground. Make sure your sage is in a sunny area that gets some shade in the evening and morning. Too much sun can burn the delicate leaves.

Water your sage plant daily but be careful not to over water. Once you see consistent growth you can water as needed.

Planting Companions and Planting Mismatches

Companions: Since sage helps to repel certain insects it does well to grow beside nearly every vegetable in the garden.

Mismatches: Cucumbers, other herbs that are very herbaceous or have strong scents

Growing and Care

The large leaves of sage enjoy sunlight however they are incredibly delicate. This is why you have to protect your Sage from the harsh midday sun. Instead allow it to sit in the early morning and the late afternoon sun.

Sage is also incredibly susceptible to overwatering. In fact it is perhaps the most susceptible herb to this. Very careful with how much you water and do not over-soak the soil. The top layer of soil should look dry or just a little moist, however when you press down on the soil you should feel the dampness. Like most other herbs feel free to put it in a pot that is well-drained so you are able to move it around your garden following the sun while still protecting it.

Tips For Pest and Disease Control

Sage is no stranger to the same pests that most other herbs attract. This means that following the same sort of pest control procedures will work for sage as it does with other herbs. For example spraying the herbs with a forceful and steady stream of water to drown and wash away bugs will work well. Organic and natural insecticides can also be sprayed on to the stage to help deter the pests from returning.

Although there are many different kinds and varieties of sage you will know that yours has been infected with a disease or infiltrated by pests because the leaves will tell you. They will no longer be bright in color, they will be wilted, and they might even begin to change their smell. Because herbs have leaves so close together it is incredibly important that you notice damage as soon as possible to help stop further issues.

Harvesting

To harvest you can either pick individual leaves from your plant or you can pull out filler sprigs from the plant. Try to take from the top first to continue to encourage regrowth. Know that if you take from the roots, that root will not regrow. Instead, if you need to take more at a time, think about cutting your plant about three to four inches above soil level.

If you find that the plant is drying out, you can always take the whole plant, dry out the leaves, and blend it to create a dry spice.

Chapter 37

Thyme

Introduction

There are a number of varieties of thyme. Each of them have different flavor notes and some can even be used as decoration instead of an actual herb. Just like other herbs that have different variations most of the species of thyme that are used as food grow under the same conditions. This means that the only difficult part of growing thyme is choosing the flavor profile you like.

Planting

Planting Instructions From Seeds or Scraps

Choose a long healthy stem from an established thyme plant. Gently pull it from the soil or cut it away from the mother plant. Remove all leaves and leave only about two inches worth of leaves at the top.

Cut the bottom of the stem at a 45 degree angle. Dip the end in growth or rooting hormone to encourage new roots. Place the herb in a small glass of water: make sure that the water is covering at least two inches of the stem, but have no leaves touching the water. Place the glass in a

sunny and warm spot - a window sill that gets full sun will do just fine for this.

Replace water as needed: you may also want to change your glass to a taller one as your herb grows.

Once you see new roots forming, and you begin to see new leaves, your thyme is ready to plant.

Plant in a pot, or the ground, with at least two inches under the soil and two inches above the soil. Water daily to make sure the plant stays moist but do not let water sit.

After you see growth on a consistent basis you can water as needed.

Planting Instructions From A Shrub

Leave the plant outside in your yard for 24-48 hours. Water it well. This will help acclimate the plant to your yard's climate.

You can keep the herb in the pot or plant in the ground: just make sure at least inches are under the soil and at least two inches are above the ground. Make sure your thyme is in a sunny area that gets some shade in the evening and morning. Too much sun can burn the delicate leaves.

Water your thyme daily, but be careful not to over water. Once you see consistent growth you can water as needed.

Planting Companions and Planting Mismatches

Companions: strawberries

Mismatches: will generally grow with everything

Growing and Care

Thyme loves sunlight however Most of the varieties are delicate and will burn under scorching sun. Therefore, as long as you protect it from the midday sun, and keep the soil moist you will likely be successful in growing it.

One aspect of growing and caring for thyme that differs slightly from other herbs isn't that its leaves are incredibly small and bunched together. Harvest often to encourage regrowth. If the thyme plant is never harvested then the leaves that are there will rot and hinder regrowth. Thankfully even if you harvest often you will be able to dry it out to elongate the life of the herb.

Tips For Pest and Disease Control

To deter pests from your thyme plant you need only to follow the same sort of procedures as you would for parsley or any other small leaf herb. Again making sure that you use a steady stream of water to drown and wash away any insects. However, be sure that the leaves are fully dry and that there is no water sitting on the plant or in the soil. Too much water will compromise the herbs ability to absorb nutrients and ultimately lead to diseases, more pests, and the failure of the plant.

Harvesting

To harvest you can either pick individual leaves from your plant or you can pull out filler sprigs from the plant. Try to take from the top first to continue to encourage regrowth.

Know that if you take from the roots, that root will not regrow. Instead, if you need to take more at a time, think about cutting your plant about three to four inches above soil level.

If you find that the plant is drying out, you can always take the whole plant, dry out the leaves, and blend it to create a dry spice.

Chapter 38

Turmeric

Introduction

Turmeric is a powerful anti-inflammatory root that has been used since ancient times. However, it is often forgotten when it comes to growing it in a garden because it is seen as difficult. While turmeric may be difficult to incorporate into meals and handle - because of the bright yellow pigment- it is quite easy to grow.

Planting

Planting Instructions From Seeds or Scraps

Soak your turmeric in water for 24 hours. This will help to wash the skin and remove preservatives from the store. Sometimes commercial Farms spray their turmeric with ani-growth hormones to stop the rhizomes from growing again. Once you've soaked the root, leave it on the counter to dry for 24 hours.

Prepare your soil by mixing in either homemade or commercial fertilizers.

Do not peel the turmeric and try to choose pieces that have 'eyes' on them. It is from these 'eyes' that new turmeric will grow. Cut the turmeric into pieces that are about one inch long. Leave these pieces out for at least 24 hours so the cut side can form a callus. This may take a few days.

Plant the turmeric about 2-4 inches under the soil with the cut side up. If you see buds forming make sure that these buds are facing towards the sky. Place your plant in a warm sunny spot; because turmeric grows under the ground it needs lots of sun.

Planting Instructions From A Shrub

Leave the plant outside in your yard for 24-48 hours. Water it well. This will help acclimate the plant to your yard's climate.

From here you can leave it in the pot, transplant it into a larger pot, or plant it into the ground. If you transplant it be sure to use a bigger pot that it came in as the plant will likely grow. Turmeric, like ginger, can grow up to three feet tall.

Planting Companions and Planting Mismatches

Companions: most bean types, cilantro, ginger, and peas

Mismatches: eggplant, tomatoes, berries

Growing and Care

Even though your turmeric root loves sun it loves water just as much. Make sure the soil stays moist but not be careful to not soak it. Sitting water is a death sentence for roots like turmeric.

Turmeric grows under the ground and will have its stems and leaves protrude above the soil. If your soil is too wet or too dry then you will have weak and wrinkly spice.

Tips For Pest and Disease Control

Like ginger, turmeric is at the mercy of those bugs that live under the soil. This can also make it harder to notice any bugs or disease.

Keep an eye on the leaves and stems that grow out of the ground. Damaged leaves, wilting stems, or discoloration are all signs that there is an infestation of insects or disease underneath.

You should feel free to spray pesticides in your garden, but be careful to choose one that is safe for humans. However, you can also release ladybugs into the garden. They will eat the smaller insects that can damage your plants.

Harvesting

To harvest turmeric you will have to pull up the entire plant. You can pull the root out by grasping the stem close to the soil surface and pull directly upwards. Another option is for you to use your hands, as tools can harm the spice, and dig into the soil about 6 inches all around the plant. Gently pull out the spice and brush off any soil that is left on it. You can harvest turmeric at any point in the growing process but it is ideal for it to be harvested about 10 months after planting. Their stems should be thick in diameter, sturdy, and standing upright.

Although you will be digging up the whole plant, you will be able to use the scraps to grow it again.

Part Five

Rooting Hormone

Chapter 39

Fertilizers

Fertilizers are a great way of enriching the soil. They can also help your soil drain better, hold on to nutrients better, and generally help to promote growth. Some fertilizers can be expensive and hard to work with. Knowing how to make your own can help bring down the cost of gardening (Huffstetler).

Epsom Salt Fertilizer

The first at home fertilizer uses Epsom salts. These salts are high in magnesium and sulfates; two nutrients and substances that are important for plant growth and food production.

Add 1 tablespoon of Epsom salt into one gallon of warm water. Shake and stir the water mixture until all of the salt is dissolved. Use this to water your plants once a month when you are waiting for the plant to establish roots.

Be very careful with how often you use the mixture and make sure you are only getting it on the soil. Epsom salts are toxic to humans in large amounts, therefore using too strong of a mixture or using it too often can lead to food that is harmful to eat. However, if you follow the above instructions you will be fine.

Coffee Ground Fertilizer

Coffee grounds as fertilizer is one of the most popular 'do it yourself' versions because they are so easy to come by. Nearly everyone has large amounts of coffee grounds on hand. To make the fertilizer, spread the grounds on a sheet pan on top of the newspaper. Allow the ground to dry out totally. This can take up to a couple days to do. To make it go by faster you can put the pan in the over at a low temperature for a few hours. However, be wary that too long in the oven can actually put more moisture back into the grounds.

Once the grounds are dried you can either mix them in with the soil, place them around the base of your individual plants, or mix them with the water you use to feed your crops.

Coffee grounds are high in nitrogen, potassium, and magnesium which can help your soil hold onto nutrients instead of washing them away with the water. Although you do have to be careful with this fertilizer. Using too much can make your soil too acidic. You should only use a small teaspoon of grounds each time and use this fertilizer only once a week or a few times per month at most. You can also test your soil to make sure that your soil stays at an acceptable acid level.

Eggshell Fertilizer

Egg shells are rich in calcium carbonate. They can provide proteins to your plants and help them absorb the nutrients from sunlight, soil, and water.

Leave your cracked eggshells on the counter for a few days. This will help to dry them out. To quicken this process you can also microwave them or throw them in the over at a low temperature for a few hours. However, leaving them on the counter is a waste and electricity free way of drying them.

No matter how you choose to do it, once the shells are dried, blend them into a sand. To use you can either spread them on top of your soil, mix them into your soil, or add the dust to the water you use to feed your plants.

Vinegar Fertilizer

Vinegar is a useful liquid in a number of areas. It is used in the kitchen for cooking, it can be used to create beautiful works of art, it can help clear acne and skin problems, and it can be used as a cleaning product. But it can also be used as a fertilizer for plants, fruits, and vegetables.

To make this fertilizer mix 1 tablespoon of plain white vinegar with warm water. You can then use this mixture to water your plants. To make this fertilizer go further you can also put it into a spray bottle and spray the base of your plants and soil.

If you choose this recipe you do need to take care and not add too much vinegar. You should also not put vinegar directly on your plants or soil. On its own vinegar is an herbicide and kills your plants.

Fish Tank Fertilizer

If you have a fish tank you can make your own fertilizer rather easily. As your fish breathe and live in the water they help to oxidize and enrich the water. Moreover, the algae that can be collected from a fish tank holds some powerful substances that can help plants grow.

The next time you change the water in your fish tank do not throw it out. Instead mix it with regular water from the hose or tap, and use it to water your plants.

Ashes Fertilizer

This kind of fertilizer is perhaps the easiest to come by as your only need to burn wood. If you are gardening you most likely already have a campfire or fireplace on your property. Wood ashes are high in potassium and calcium; two chemicals that can help to balance the acidity and ph levels of the ground. It can also help your plants to absorb the nutrients it needs to thrive.

Simply gather the ashes, if they are larger you can blend them or crush them into dust. Then sprinkle them directly onto the soil, or mix them into the soil.

You do not want to add these to water like some of the other fertilizers as it can be counterproductive to your goal. Also be sure they can come from a true wood burning fire. Ashes from food fires, or fires that contain other substances like plastics or paper will not work.

Do It Yourself Compost

Compost is a great way of adding nutrients to your soil. To do so, add all organic and food scraps into a compost safe bin. Every time you add more food scraps be sure to mix the scraps to help incorporate them all together.

As the food scraps decompose they will create a soil and mucky like substance. You can either mix this in with your soil while planting or place it on top of the soil at the base of your plants.

Composting does have its downfalls. It takes some time for the food to break down and it does take some labor as you have to mix and stir the mixture. Thankfully you can get composting containers that spin and circulate the mixture for you. Composting can also be toxic. As the food breaks down it gives off different kinds of gas. Be sure to buy a proper compost bin to protect yourself and your compost.

Compost Tea

To make compost tea, simply add your scraps to a bucket of water. Make sure that your compost is all food scraps. Don't include paper or compostable paper substances. Leave the bucket outside in the sun for 24-48 hours. The heat will help pull the nutrients out of the food and mix with the water.

After the compost steps you can strain the water. Either toss the scraps or add them to your traditional composting bin. Use the water to water your plants as it will add more nutrients as well as be hydrating for you plants. You will not want to drink this and it can be toxic to humans if ingested directly.

In the end these fertilizers are incredibly successful and helpful to enrich the soil in your gardens; in the Florida climate any added nutrients is always a bonus. Of course, there is an environmental aspect to making your own fertilizers as well. You will be cutting down on your own food scraps as you are reusing your food scraps instead of simply throwing them out.

To cut down on cost, help your food grow, and help the environment, there is really no reason to not fertilize your plants.

Chapter 40

Pest Control

As we've mentioned many times over in the book, pests and bugs are one of the largest reasons that plants do not thrive, or fruits and vegetables don't sprout. The easiest way to counter the number of different pests, is to spray your plants with different insecticides. Unfortunately there are significant downfalls to the commercial sprays. First they can be expensive. Secondly they can be tricky to use. In fact if used improperly some of these insecticides can actually be harmful to both the plant and to the human to eat the food. A third downfall is that they create quite a bit of waste both in their production and in the empty bottles they leave. For this reason, making your own insecticides has become incredibly popular (Markham, 2021).

Vegetable Oil

Vegetable oil is a useful insecticide because it stops small aphids and mites from attaching themselves to your plant and eating it. To make this spray combine 1 cup of vegetable oil and a single tablespoon of a liquid soap. Keep this mixture in an airtight container on the counter for up to a month.

To use, add 2 tablespoons of this oil soap mixture to about a quart of water. Stir this mixture until you cannot tell the difference between the two liquids. You need only to spray your plants liberally with this mixture. You can spray the leaves, the stems comment or the soil itself. If the insects have not found your plant yet it will help to deter that however if they are already there it will help to suffocate them.

Soap

Using soap as an insecticide will deter insects as they won't be able to grab on to the leaves and stems. To make this mixture combine one and a half teaspoons of a liquid soap with a full court of water. Shake and stir this mixture until you cannot differentiate between the two liquids.

Feel free to spray this all over your plants and at the base of their stems.

Garlic

Take two whole bulbs of garlic and make them into a paste by blending them with a few tablespoons of water. Allow this paste to sit overnight and strain it into a large container. Then add half a cup of vegetable oil, 1 tsp of liquid soap, and enough water to make a full court of the mixture. Stir this combination well until it becomes one.

You can then spray this directly onto the plants or base of your crops. This insecticide works because many pests are deterred by the strong smell of garlic.

Chile Pepper

Add one tablespoon of chili powder to 1 quart of water. Then add a few drops of liquid soap to the mixture. Shake and stir this combination well until everything is fully combined. If you do not have chili powder you can make this spray with fresh chili peppers. Puree half a cup of chili peppers into 1 cup of water. Add this to a quart of water and boil it until the mixture thickens and becomes fully combined. Allow the mixture to cool before adding the liquid soap then feel free to use and spray as you wish. You can then spray this mixture onto your plants directly.

Be careful however, chili peppers tend to be very powerful and potent for humans. When spraying make sure you spray away from your eyes, and make sure you do not touch your eyes when making the spray itself.

Garlic, Onion, Cayenne Pepper and Hand Soap

This insecticide is perhaps the one that is most laborious to make as it includes multiple ingredients. Chop and puree an entire bulb of garlic.

Add that with one diced small onion and a teaspoon of cayenne pepper. Place all of these ingredients into a quart of water and allow the mixture to steep and marinate for 1 hour. Once the hour has elapsed, strain the mixture and add 1 tbsp of liquid hand soap. Shake and mix this combination well.

Now you need only to spray it directly onto the leaves of your plants. You can even spray this to the underside of the plant to have full coverage.

Make sure that you compost the garlic and onion mixture to have zero waste to produce this spray.

Tomato

Tomatoes contain alkaloids that help to repel aphids and other insects of the same kind. To make this spray you need only to chop up tomato leaves until you have about two cups. Specifically you want the leaves from the tomato plant and not necessarily from the top of the tomato itself.

Mix these two cups of tomato leaves into one quart of water and allow them to steep overnight or for 24 hours. Once fully steeped you need only to strain the leaves from the water. This water can then be sprayed as needed onto your fruits and vegetables. The leftover leaves can then be put in your compost to have zero waste.

By making your own pest control spray you can help deter different insects from your plans while avoiding any harm to yourself. You'll already have the ingredients. Therefore, they are less expensive to make and use, and are more environmentally friendly as they are made out of organic substances.

When paired with the at home fertilizers discussed in the previous chapter, these at home Pest Control Spray can make your garden thrive and have a bountiful harvest year after year.

Chapter 41

Rooting Hormone

Throw the book we've spoken about rooting hormones. Essentially what this is a serum or substance that encourages new routes to come out of seas, stems, and cuttings. Rooting hormone is commercially available at any greenhouse, garden center, or even hardware store. However, they can be expensive and the ingredients can be chemically based. When it comes to growing your own food you want to know what is going into your plans. This is why we suggest that you make your own rooting hormone.

Honey Rooting Hormone

Honey is an incredibly healthy substance for both humans and plants. For this rooting hormone you're going to want to use organic and raw honey if you can find it. Although processed honey works relatively well, more success has been found with raw organic honey. The more processed the honey has the more additives are in it. This means that you aren't getting the true benefit of the honey when you use it as a rooting hormone.

Once you've gathered your honey, bring 2 cups of water to a boil. Using 1 tbsp at a time, take the boiling water and add it to the honey. The water will help break up and loosen the honey a little bit. You do not want to totally dilute the honey just enough so it becomes a little bit more of a gel or a syrupy consistency.

To use it you simply need to dip your cut end of your stem into the honey. Make sure the honey quotes about half an inch to an inch of the stem fully. Then plant your cutting as per its specific planting and growing instructions. Put the honey liquid in an airtight container to store.

Aloe Vera Rooting Hormone

Harvest in aloe vera leaf. You should have the pointed end closed and where you cut the aloe vera open. Place the aloe vera on the table and with a spoon gently apply pressure from the pointed end down to the cut end. In doing so this will push all of the gel within the aloe vera leave out.

Put this gel in a small cup and stir your aloe vera to break up any checks. The end result should be a smooth gel like consistency. You need only now to dip your cut stem into the aloe vera and coat about half an inch to an inch of it. Then follow the other propagating or growing instructions for that specific plant.

Some people dip their stem directly into the cut end of the aloe vera. While this takes less steps and is less messy it is inconsistent. Aloe vera by nature is gel-like and a little chunky. If you dip your stem into the aloe vera leaf you might not get full coverage or coding. It is best to take it out and stir it to break up the chunks before dipping your stem.

Cinnamon Rooting Hormone

Cinnamon is a powerful spice and antioxidant that can encourage growth and health from cuttings. To make this rooting hormone take a tablespoon of cinnamon and place it on a paper towel. You want to make sure that the cinnamon is ground. You can purchase organic ground cinnamon or you can ground cinnamon yourself from the bark.

Take your cuttings or your stem, that you have already cut at a 45 degree angle, and dip it in a little bit of water to moisten the end: you will want about half an inch of the stem wet.

Then roll the stem in the cinnamon making sure that the cinnamon is covering all the way around the stem and the cut area.

Then follow the propagating or planting instructions for the specific plant.

Rooting hormone is an alternative substance and aspect of growing food in a garden. It is not necessary. However, it can make an incredible difference in how well your plants grow, especially when you grow them from scraps or cutting. Since the Florida climate can be a little merciless and fickle, any help you can get to make your garden successful you should take. And since he's rooting hormones are easy to make with things that you probably already have in your home, there is no reason not to use them (*Homemade rooting hormone* 2022).

Final Thoughts

Throughout this book we have discussed arrangement formation associated with gardening in Florida. We've talked about how to start a garden and how to successfully face the specific challenges of the Florida climate. We've gone through a number of different fruits, vegetables and other types of food and how they can be grown in Florida successfully. Lastly we have provided a number of recipes and concoctions you can make in your own home to help encourage growth and provide a healthy harvest for your garden.

It is important to note that while this information is extensive it is by no means exhaustive. For example the challenges we named for growing in Florida are not all that there are. Individuals have a number of different challenges that are specific to their backyard climate. We have simply summarized the most popular and general challenges. Likewise the recipes we have given you are not the only options out there. Fertilizers can come from nearly every sort of natural organic substance: rooting hormones and insecticides have hundreds of different recipes available. Lastly, the list of fruits and vegetables we've provided is not complete. These are by no means all of the foods that you can grow in your backyard in the state of Florida. To create such a book would be an endless exercise in repetition.

Instead what we have provided to you is enough information for you to get your garden started, grow your fruits and vegetables successfully, and extrapolate on the information to other fruits and vegetables. We've gone through so many different families, food and growing conditions that you will be hard-pressed to find one not on the list that has a completely different set of growing instructions.

If we can give you one more piece of advice before we send you on your way it would be to take your time. You do not need to plant every single fruit and vegetable all at once. Start with some of the more easy ones to understand and the ones that are more likely to be successful. For example herbs and spices can grow in almost any growing conditions. You can start there. You can start with a simple tomato or cucumber plant. No matter where you start we suggest starting small. Get your hands dirty so to speak and then move on from there as you get more comfortable.

We are urging you to move forward and take this book as a sort of reference guide for your adventure into gardening. Gardening is a wonderful pastime that can provide a sense of confidence and accomplishment that many individuals would otherwise lack.

Gardening is about creating something and nurturing it as it grows. It is not meant to be stressful or frustrating. Make sure you enjoy the journey and the fruits of your labor.

References

20 plants not to grow under a black walnut tree. Tree Journey. (2022, January 14). Retrieved August 15, 2022, from https://treejourney.com/plants-not-to-plant-under-a-black-walnut-tree/

Annie, & How to Establish a Fantastic Edible Food Forest Easily - 15 Acre Homestead. (2017, April 2). *The top 10 Florida gardening challenges*. 15 Acre Homestead. Retrieved August 19, 2022, from https://15acrehomestead.com/florida-gardening-challenges/

Bailey, M. (2020, November 28). *Unique challenges of growing in North Central florida*. Gainesville Sun. Retrieved August 19, 2022, from https://www.gainesville.com/story/lifestyle/2020/11/28/unique-challenges-growing-north-central-florida/6424034002/

Bailey, M. (2020, November 28). *Unique challenges of growing in North Central florida*. Gainesville Sun. Retrieved August 19, 2022, from https://www.gainesville.com/story/lifestyle/2020/11/28/unique-challenges-growing-north-central-florida/6424034002/

Beginners Guide to Companion Planting. Heeman's. (2022, May 11). Retrieved August 19, 2022, from https://heeman.ca/garden-guides/companion-planting/

Blackberries. Blackberries - Gardening Solutions - University of Florida, Institute of Food and Agricultural Sciences. (n.d.). Retrieved August 15, 2022, from https://gardeningsolutions.ifas.ufl.edu/plants/edibles/fruits/blackberries.html#:~:text=Plant%20your%20blackberry%20plants%20from,minimize%20weeds%2C%20as%20will%20mulch.

Blackberry propagation: Growing blackberries from cuttings. (n.d.). Retrieved August 15, 2022, from https://www.gardeningknowhow.com/edible/fruits/blackberries/propagating-blackberries-cuttings.htm

Blueberry Bush: Planting, care, pruning and harvesting instructions. Blueberry Care Instructions. (n.d.). Retrieved August 15, 2022, from https://www.arborday.org/trees/fruit/care-blueberry.cfm#:~:text=Deep%2C%20low%20pH%20mulch%20like,per%20week%20during%20fruit%20ripening.

Citrus pests. Agriculture and Food. (n.d.). Retrieved August 15, 2022, from https://www.agric.wa.gov.au/pest-insects/citrus-pests

Citrus. Citrus - Gardening Solutions - University of Florida, Institute of Food and Agricultural Sciences. (n.d.). Retrieved August 15, 2022, from https://gardeningsolutions.ifas.ufl.edu/plants/edibles/fruits/citrus.html#:~:text=Most%20well%2Ddrained%20potting%20soils,stray%20branches%20or%20lower%20limbs.

Climate - Florida (United States). Florida climate: weather by month, temperature, precipitation, when to go. (n.d.). Retrieved August 19, 2022, from https://www.climatestotravel.com/climate/united-states/florida#:~:text=In%20much%20of%20Florida%2C%20the,muggy%20and%20with%20frequent%20thunderstorms.

Costa Farms. North and Central Florida Gardening Guide | Costa Farms. (n.d.). Retrieved August 19, 2022, from https://www.costafarms.com/get-growing/news/north-and-central-florida-gardening-guide

Editors, R. S. (2022, June 3). *Start-a-garden checklist*. Real Simple. Retrieved August 19, 2022, from https://www.realsimple.com/home-organizing/gardening/outdoor/garden-starting-checklist

Florida Weekly Staff | on May 20, 2020. (2020, May 28). *It Ain't easy being green: The challenge of gardening in Florida - fort myers Florida weekly*. Fort Myers Florida Weekly -. Retrieved August 19, 2022, from https://fortmyers.floridaweekly.com/articles/it-aint-easy-being-green-the-challenge-of-gardening-in-florida/

Ginger pest problems: Dealing with bugs that eat ginger plants. (n.d.). Retrieved August 19, 2022, from https://www.gardeningknowhow.com/ornamental/flowers/ornamental-ginger/ginger-insect-problems.htm

Growing Blueberries. Blueberries - Gardening Solutions - University of Florida, Institute of Food and Agricultural Sciences. (n.d.). Retrieved August 15, 2022, from https://gardeningsolutions.ifas.ufl.edu/plants/edibles/fruits/blueberries.html

Harvesting banana plants - stark bro's. Stark Bro's Nurseries & Orchards Co. (n.d.). Retrieved August 15, 2022, from https://www.starkbros.com/growing-guide/how-to-grow/fruit-trees/banana-plants/harvesting

Homemade rooting hormone. Juggling Act Mama. (2022, June 9). Retrieved August 15, 2022, from https://www.jugglingactmama.com/homemade-rooting-hormone-3-ways/

Hoover, E. E. (n.d.). *Growing stone fruits in the Home Garden*. UMN Extension. Retrieved August 19, 2022, from https://extension.umn.edu/fruit/growing-stone-fruits-home-garden#harvesting-and-storing-fruit-1136561

How to grow hardy banana plants. Arts Nursery Ltd | Garden Centre and Nursery. (n.d.). Retrieved August 15, 2022, from https://www.artsnursery.com/article/how-to-grow-hardy-banana-plants#:~:text=Banana%20plants%20prefer%20to%20be,fountains%20or%20mist%20them%20occasionally.

How to tell when a watermelon is ripe: 6 testing methods - 2022. MasterClass. (n.d.). Retrieved August 15, 2022, from https://www.masterclass.com/articles/how-to-tell-when-a-watermelon-is-ripe

How to tell when melons are ripe: Gardener's supply. www.gardeners.com. (n.d.). Retrieved August 15, 2022, from https://www.gardeners.com/how-to/when-melons-are-ripe/7967.html

HS2/MG216: Mango growing in the Florida Home Landscape. (n.d.). Retrieved August 15, 2022, from https://edis.ifas.ufl.edu/publication/MG216

Huffstetler, E. (n.d.). *Use these 7 homemade fertilizer recipes in your garden*. The Spruce. Retrieved August 15, 2022, from https://www.thespruce.com/make-your-own-fertilizer-1388159#:~:text=Combine%201%20tablespoon%20of%20white,thing%20-for%20acid%2Dloving%20plants.

Josh. (2019, June 30). *Best fruit trees to grow in Florida (14 easy to grow trees)*. FL Gardening. Retrieved August 19, 2022, from https://www.flgardening.com/best-fruit-trees-to-grow-in-florida/#:~:text=Apples%2C%20Avocado%2C%20Bananas%2C%20Citrus,temperate%20climate%20here%20in%20Florida.

Josh. (2020, May 29). *27 easy vegetables to grow in Florida: For all parts of the State*. FL Gardening. Retrieved August 19, 2022, from https://www.flgardening.com/27-vegetables-that-grow-easily-in-florida/

Josh. (2020, May 29). *Florida Vegetable Gardening: A complete beginners guide*. FL Gardening. Retrieved August 19, 2022, from https://www.flgardening.com/florida-vegetable-gardening/

Leaf Group. (n.d.). *Grapes to grow in Florida.* eHow. Retrieved August 15, 2022, from https://www.ehow.com/info_8137934_grapes-grow-florida.html

Levin, J. (n.d.). How to grow autoflowers outside. Retrieved August 15, 2022, from https://apotforpot.com/blogs/growing/autoflowers-outdoors/

Markham, D. (2021, April 6). *8 natural & Homemade Insecticides: Save your garden without killing the Earth.* Treehugger. Retrieved August 15, 2022, from https://www.treehugger.com/natural-homemade-insecticides-save-your-garden-without-killing-earth-4858819

Must have Florida plants – best plants for Florida gardening. (n.d.). Retrieved August 19, 2022, from https://www.gardeningknowhow.com/special/must-have-florida-plants.htm

Neverman, L. (2022, June 30). *How to start a garden – 10 steps to gardening for Beginners.* Common Sense Home. Retrieved August 19, 2022, from https://commonsense-home.com/start-a-garden/

Planting and caring for nut trees - lrconline.com. (n.d.). Retrieved August 15, 2022, from http://www.lrconline.com/Extension_Notes_English/pdf/////nut_trs.pdf

Preventing apple pests. HGTV. (n.d.). Retrieved August 19, 2022, from https://www.hgtv.com/outdoors/flowers-and-plants/fruit/preventing-apple-pests

SL441/SS655: Agricultural soils of Florida. (n.d.). Retrieved August 19, 2022, from https://edis.ifas.ufl.edu/publication/ss655

Tips & information about bananas - gardening know how. (n.d.). Retrieved August 15, 2022, from https://www.gardeningknowhow.com/edible/fruits/banana

VanZile, J. (2022, February 25). *Growing papaya indoors as a houseplant.* The Spruce. Retrieved August 15, 2022, from https://www.thespruce.com/grow-papaya-indoors-1902490#:~:text=To%20sprout%20papaya%20seeds%2C%20place,contain-ers%20to%20grow%20as%20houseplants.

Vegetable gardening by season. Vegetable Gardening by Season - Gardening Solutions - University of Florida, Institute of Food and Agricultural Sciences. (n.d.). Retrieved August 19, 2022, from https://gardeningsolutions.ifas.ufl.edu/care/planting/vegetable-gardens-by-season.html

What gardening supplies do you need to grow a vegetable garden? Millcreek Garden. (2018, February 14). Retrieved August 19, 2022, from https://www.millcreekgardens.com/what-gardening-supplies-do-you-need-to-grow-a-vegetable-garden/

Will, M. (2021, October 6). *How to grow mango from seed (easy method).* Empress of Dirt. Retrieved August 15, 2022, from https://empressofdirt.net/grow-mango-seed/

Will, M. (2022, January 22). *How to grow lemon trees from seed (& other citrus fruits).* Empress of Dirt. Retrieved August 15, 2022, from https://empressofdirt.net/grow-citrus-seed/#how-to

Yes, you can grow a garden of vegetables in Florida; here's how. Tampa Bay Times. (n.d.). Retrieved August 19, 2022, from https://www.tampabay.com/things-to-do/food/cooking/yes-you-can-grow-a-garden-of-vegetables-in-florida-heres-how/2242565/#:~:text=Some%20gardeners%20like%20to%20grow,pep-pers%20and%20herbs%20can%20grow.

Image Credit: Shutterstock.com

www.ingramcontent.com/pod-product-compliance
Lightning Source LLC
Chambersburg PA
CBHW020235130626
46549CB00005B/1903